# HOW TO PROCEED

By the same author

## POETRY

*Lives*
*The Caught Sky*
*The Flower Industry*
*Brushing the Dark*
*Album of Domestic Exiles*
*Russian Ink*
*The Islanders*
*The Unmapped Page – Selected Poems*
*Tremors – New & Selected Poems*
*Speed & Other Liberties*
*Fuel*
*The Lives and Times of the Islanders*
*The Bicycle Thief & Other Poems*

## ANTHOLOGIES

*First Rights – a Decade of Island Magazine*
  (with Michael Denholm)
*Toads*

# HOW TO PROCEED

## ESSAYS

### Andrew Sant

in association with Puncher and Wattmann, Australia

All rights reserved. No part of this work covered by the copyright hereon may be reproduced or used in any means – graphic, electronic, or mechanical, including copying, recording, taping, or information storage and retrieval systems – without written permission of the publisher.

Printed by imprintdigital
Upton Pyne, Exeter
www.imprintdigital.net

Typeset by narrator
www.narrator.me.uk
info@narrator.me.uk
033 022 300 39

Published by Shoestring Press
19 Devonshire Avenue, Beeston, Nottingham, NG9 1BS, UK
(0115) 925 1827
www.shoestringpress.co.uk

First published 2015
© Copyright: Andrew Sant

The moral right of the author has been asserted.

ISBN 978-1-910323-22-9

# ACKNOWLEDGEMENTS

'On Consuming Durables' was first published in *Kill Your Darlings* (online) 2013.

'On Only Children' was first published in *Island* (No. 100) in 2005.

'On My Lasting Relationship with DH Lawrence' was first published in *Poetry in the Blood* edited by Tony Roberts (Shoestring Press, 2014).

'On Taking Risks' was first published in *Antipodes* (Vol. 25 No. 1) in 2011.

'On Being in the Company of the Writer, Geoff Dean' was first published in *Famous Reporter* (No. 43) in 2010.

'On Marriage' was first published in *Meanjin* (No. 4/2009) and then in *Best Australian Essays 2010* edited by Robert Drewe.

'On Being Transported' was first published in *Island* (No.131) in 2012.

'On Self-knowledge' was first published in *The Griffith Review* (No. 33) in 2011 and then in *Best Australian Essays 2011* edited by Ramona Koval.

# ABOUT THE AUTHOR

Andrew Sant was born in London. He emigrated with his parents to Melbourne where he completed his education. He has subsequently lived in London at various times, including much of the last decade. During this time he was Writing Fellow at the Universities of Leicester, Chichester and London (Goldsmiths College). In 2001 he was writer-in-residence at the University of Peking in Beijing, China. He jointly founded and edited for ten years the Tasmanian-based quarterly, *Island*. Parallel occupations have included work as a teacher, copywriter and arts consultant. He is a former member of the Literature Board of the Australia Council. Among the most recent of his collections of poetry are *Tremors – New and Selected Poems* (Black Pepper, Melbourne, 2004), *Speed and Other Liberties* (Salt Publishing, Cambridge UK, 2008), *Fuel* (Black Pepper, Melbourne, 2009), *The Lives and Times of the Islanders* (Shoestring Press, Nottingham, UK, 2009) and the *Bicycle Thief & Other Poems* (Black Pepper, Melbourne, 2013). In 2003 he was awarded the Centenary Medal by the Australian Government for 'his outstanding contribution to literature and education'. He now lives in Melbourne.

# CONTENTS

Foreword   1

On Consuming Durables   5
On Only Children   12
On Birdwatching   17
On Discovering How to Proceed   19
On Airports   27
On My Lasting Relationship with D.H. Lawrence   31
On Taking Risks   44
On Being in the Company of the Writer, Geoff Dean   48
On Marriage   50
On Employment   57
On Walking   77
On Time   83
On Trust   91
On Being Transported   105
On Self-knowledge   117
On Curiosity   121

Appendix   127

# FOREWORD

Mid-way through 2004 I received a request by email to contribute to the 100th anniversary issue of *Island*, the Tasmanian-based literary journal. The then editor, David Owen, was sending out similar requests to former editors of the mag I'd co-founded in 1979. I replied that I'd be happy to send him a poem, my stock-in-trade. No, he wrote back, I don't want a poem – though I never found out what he had against poems – I'd like a prose contribution. I briskly emailed back to Hobart from London where at the time I was living. What about? Anything, he said.

I recalled the last time this had been tried on me was in my final year of secondary school. It was in an English class and the teacher, a Mr Kerr (though surely it should have been spelt 'cur') asked us students to each produce an essay on a subject of our choice. I decided an informal approach would be suitable to write about a sub-species of sociability with which I'd recently been in the thick of: a Saturday night party, possibly a birthday one, I forget. But I remember that this type of party, new to me, had evolved some memorable characteristics. It had alcohol. It had rock music. It had girls in short skirts. After Kerr had handed back the essays – mine, oddly, without a mark or comment – he asked me to read my effort aloud to the class. This was boys only, they quickly warmed to my liberties with the subject and collectively responded with raucous mirth. Not so the guy in the black gown, still worn in those days in Melbourne, who I initially thought must have chosen my essay for its merits. He, no modernist, uncheerfully informed the class of the many things that were wrong with my particular work and why it, alone, had failed. Presumably, the rest of the class who had comfortably passed could further learn from my failings.

My immediate reaction to this assault is not relevant here. What is must be the fact that I vividly recalled this incident decades later. Nevertheless, with a duty to be performed and nothing to lose – a kind rejection would not have been the end of the world – I now proceeded to write. Before long I had five pieces. I'd find myself waiting, say, for a train in an underground station making notes on scraps of paper about what I'd write next. To my surprise, I was seized by the task. It had its own volition. David Owen, spoilt for choice, chose to publish 'On Only Children'. The others, also in this collection, are 'On Marriage', 'On Birdwatching', 'On Airports' and 'On Walking'.

This book would not exist, I am certain, were it not for the request to contribute to the anniversary issue. There was to be another spur – another editor to whom I am grateful. But this was considerably later, in 2009. As far as I was concerned, after I'd completed five-fold the anniversary task, that was that. The remaining pieces were destined for the bottom draw only, capacious for many writers. Then I happened upon a latest issue of the Melbourne-based journal *Meanjin*. It had a new editor, Sophie Cunningham. In the table of contents, under the heading 'Essays', there were a generous number of contributions. Nowadays, the word 'essay' has for many a formal, antiquated, earnest ring to it (in my day we stuck to 'articles' in *Island*) though of course originally when Montaigne, the first and most enduring of essayists, used the word *essai* to describe his work, this was far from the case. I was, finally, on side with the teacher, Kerr, since what I'd written in 2004 and later would go on to write didn't now seem to me to categorically identify themselves as essays. Too apparently offhand, informal, digressive and unashamedly personal. However after I'd read the copy of *Meanjin* and seen that these attributes might not offend Sophie Cunningham – who seemed to have the broadest possible view of what an essay might be – I opened the bottom drawer (so to speak) and dusted off in Melbourne what I'd written in London. She published, with expert editorial intervention, 'On Marriage'. Category in the magazine: Essays.

Now, in this collection, there are sixteen. 'On Marriage' went on to appear in the annual *Best Australian Essays* (there's no escaping the word) anthology, an encouraging surprise at the time when, back in London, I thought I'd write some more prose, unrequested, and see if I could proceed once again – a decided liberty to take.

Melbourne 2014

# ON CONSUMING DURABLES

Charity shops they're called in the UK, opportunity shops here in Australia – both run by charitable organisations, they sell donated goods: it isn't possible that there can be more fascinating shops than these. There are, I guess, plenty of people who have never entered one, never given them a thought. If some of these hypothetical people were recently listening to the BBC World News at the same time as I was while preparing lunch one early afternoon – insomniacs they'd have to be in the UK – they might have been even more surprised than me to hear that a parliamentary committee has recommended to the British Government that it restrict the number of charity shops in any one high street. Charity shops a threat to social order? So it seems. The impulse on the part of the non-charity shop frequenting listener might well have been to get down to one as quickly as possible to see what's going on – before they're possibly banned altogether. I wasn't tuned in at lunchtime the next day, a Sunday, to hear of any further developments – social order, one hoped, prevailed along the high streets in the dead of night, Greenwich meantime.

The rationale for restricting the number of charity shops – by limiting rate relief – was based on the fact that during these economically difficult times – debt, unemployment, anxiety, unrest all high – these shops are booming. They're attracting bargain-hunting customers as never before, in numbers that neighbouring commercial retailers, now struggling, can only dream of. The charity shops are copping some blame for this – directly hurting the retailers of the new and therefore in turn worsening the economic doldrums. In short, they are a drag on product churn. I hope this barmy idea doesn't find expression, a lobby group, here. For this hope I must declare a personal interest: I have at times been an enthusiastic user of charity/opportunity shops. Not an addict of them exactly, like some in my social orbit, but on the fringes of addiction, if that is what popping in occasionally – irresistibly if passing by – to satisfy my curiosity amounts to. In other words, restricting their industrious and good work would not cause in me unmanageable agitation. Though I'm equally sure such action would not more frequently lead me to speed though doors receiving insufficient use in the commercial retail sector.

When I enter the nearest opportunity shop – a ten minute bike ride from where I'm currently living in an inner suburb of Melbourne, a concern for the needy or the far off starving is not at the forefront of my mind, even though the organisation which runs the shop is named after the patron saint of the poor. The Brotherhood of St Lawrence has been creating opportunities since 1930. When I enter, I'm wondering what useful or, even, useless artefacts I'll spot and, if so driven, buy. I may then have faintly remembered that my cash is not profiting some monster company which covertly runs sweat shops in a developing nation.

The Brotherhood opportunity shop, in a semi-industrial zone, is actually the size of a large warehouse, so there's a lot of territory to cover, and a lot of donated stuff regularly arriving by truck at the back entrance. The blokes who unload it are full of blarney and bluster. No problems there with workplace relations. They unload clothes, furniture, books, electrical goods, paintings and prints, white goods, sporting equipment, crockery, records and CDs, millinery, knick-knacks galore – pretty much whatever durables in working order can be lifted into and out of a truck. The size of what I can manageably transport is normally restricted by the fact that I've arrived by bike and therefore what I can fit into my backpack: books (occasionally first editions!), rare old records, small paintings – a couple, finely executed by anonymous artists, now on my wall – wooden picture frames, earthenware items, and the like.

Once, for a couple of weeks, I binged and furnished the studio apartment where I recurrently live. This required a van and the added strength of a friend. The occasion: I'd moved back to Melbourne, leaving behind me a leased, furnished house. My second set of furniture needed to be found quickly – at the

Brotherhood it was all to be found under one roof – and cheaply: easy, should the time come, to jettison it. I gave myself a budget of a low, low $500 – lower than the average weekly wage. There could be a reality TV show for a challenge of this kind: furnish a house for five hundred bucks, the winner being the contestant who accomplishes the feat in the most stylish fashion. In my eyes, after all of the lifting and shifting, I reckon I'd have been in the running for the final. I was especially pleased with the black leather couch and an armless easy chair, probably made in the 60s, reflecting Bauhaus design – and no-one with any taste could possibly sneer at the rectangular tables. Or, for that matter, at any of the other fine items we manipulated into position. But I kept the place TV free: more reality about without one. Then, having achieved my aim, I blew it, and began handing over sums of money not destined for charity. For a hand-woven Pakistani kilim, a late nineteenth-century Chinese low table, should there ever be an occasion to take tea with guests, sitting on the floor, cross-legged – and then I bought a large painting, after a sudden rush of blood to the head at an exhibition opening, by a leading Australian artist I've long admired. The cost of the whole enterprise had now rocketed into the stratospheric region of five figures. But still, in the proximity of these luxury items, and to emphasise the quality and range of goods available at the Brotherhood shop, the furniture still looked great – the comfortable chairs suitable for sitting back and appreciating the painting.

Furniture dominates much of the back of the Brotherhood shop – clothes much of the front. The French disapprove of bargain-hunters moving in on goods considered, in their equivalently styled and stocked shops, to be reserved for the poor. Here and in the UK the doors are cheerfully open to all who'll generate income for charity and with extra thanks added should a happy customer refuse her change, one donation attracting another. These are not gloomy places. From among the long rows of clothes racks at the Brotherhood shop you can often hear laughter, even shrieks of surprise from women of several ages delighted to have spotted a retro chic item – a dress perhaps one of their aunts might have taken very seriously. Younger women, with brightly dyed hair and pale faces, explode through the changing booth curtains to show off a sudden combo of clothes whose juxtaposition would be assured to make some aunts nonplussed. Men, in their section, generally keep their emotions in check, so one can only guess at the strength of any subterranean eruption of delight at a find, say, a tie. The fact is, every deeply satisfied customer knows that the staff who price the items – a Bauhaus-style chair for ten dollars, a women's twin set from the 'swinging sixties' for twenty – have no eye for a truly valuable item. At least that's the experience on a good day, since the bargain-hunter must have beaten the opportunistic second-hand dealers – always one or two possibly about – to find it.

These fascinating places – often large-scale in Australia, small (but threatening) as befits high street shop fronts in the UK – bring out our primitive impulses to hunt. Think bison, think leather couch. These impulses don't on an average day at any particular urban postcode get sufficient chance to be satisfied. Another thing: the moaning UK commercial retail outlets could learn a thing or two from charity shops, especially with regard to clothes. Goodness, they've had long enough to do so: Oxfam, the first of the charity shops, has been around since 1947. When living in north London, I can't resist the opportunity to frequently check out the nearest, not because I want to bag a bargain for the sake of it – the consumerist trap – but because of the choice and quality of the apparel. In middle-market Gap clothes shops, to provide a representative example, the range (if it can so be called) of clothes is confined to the style settings of the current season, take or leave it, and try to forget the third world factories where the single-label stuff likely originates. In charity shops the seasons are many and varied, from the recent and going back to, well, possibly all the way back to 1947. So no one set of styles is imposed on the customer who, if he is me, is not inclined to be trapped in a product straightjacket. Furthermore, the variety of brands is without bounds. Examples: I have an Italian-made Armani jacket without having had to tap my bank manager for an extra line of credit, and another jacket, now gracing one of my coat hangers, by Thomas Nash – also a natty brown corduroy suit and on its label the maker, Harrods. The beneficiary: charity. Admittedly, the shop I go to is located within a fairly classy demographic but if members of it choose to discard a recent season's clothes still in the state in which they first went on display in some posh shop, then go out to buy more that's their business. The parliamentary committee, recommending the restrictions, would I am sure congratulate such customers on their absurd lust for consumption.

One of the most successful baggers of pre-loved or re-loved attire in the north London neighbourhood that supplies the charity shop I go to is a famous English actress with a pedigree which comes with a double-barrel surname (but super classy, no hyphen) and establishment connections. Her award-winning performances are mostly in period dramas where, swanning about aristocratically, she's dolled up in the most elegant-looking outfits suitable for the time. Out on the high street, now, close to where she lives, it's a different matter. So much so, that I didn't immediately recognise her. She goes in for what I would perhaps ignorantly describe as a gothic look, emphasis black, hair in attractive disarray. My theory was that she dressed down, covered her petite and desirable person in unruly rag-tag gear to avoid being spotted and therefore gain the personal freedom that comes with anonymity. I thought I'd done well, spotting her while pretending not to. This became quite regular on the busy high street now that I was savvy to her game. Way back, when my mother – who had an eye for elegant outfits – was approximately the actress's age and I was still in lovingly pressed shorts, wearing an item of clothing that had adorned a previous owner was considered to be 'common'. Hand-me-downs were *our* privilege to hand down. I don't know who we thought we were, living – as we did – in a modest semi-detached house in an outer-London suburb, but I did know there was a lot, and ever growing list, of 'common' behaviour about. I was made aware of this because I brought some of it home. Now here was a member of an establishment family, the sort of family which we presumably once looked up to, exhibiting the very kind of street behaviour, fancy free, we looked down upon.

How times change! But from where, I wondered, from which recycled clothing shop run I supposed by a charity – maybe the Heart Foundation or Save the Children – did this pretty woman get her remarkable gear? I don't check out the women's racks, so maybe I'd missed the availability. I brought the matter up with a friend of mine who, as former curator of dress at London's Victoria and Albert Museum, would surely be interested. She was enlightening. My mother would have been pleased to hear her words – so would the parliamentary committee. I'd provided the actress with a role she didn't know she was playing in a kind of shop she'd quite possibly never entered. In short – and if I bothered with celebrity news in the media or owned a TV, I might have known this – her memorable attire, its apparently scruffy unironed dark folds and frills, was bought new. Designer-made. Possibly one-offs. Truly expensive. This goes to show that, in my eyes at least, there's not a scrap of difference, appearance-wise, between getting about in haute couture and the latest bargain from Oxfam. Perhaps the actress, after some heady opening night, treading the red carpet in mismatched shoes, and now weary of her latest, new, over-photographed outfit has, on a whim, let it go. I can visualise the kind of thing hanging on a rack in the kind of shop I recently, naively, assumed she frequented, and, pinned on its sleeve, the charity shop price tag shows it's going for a song – and who cares about the identity of its former owner.

The parliamentary committee would be pleased to hear that in the UK I don't restrict my own clothes shopping to such shops, though it might be unhappy to hear that, no matter what the outlet, I don't buy much. Someone who leads a peripatetic life, as I do, is not likely to be a keen accumulator, a virtuous consumer. Had the committee, I wondered while listening to the BBC World News on the radio, considered the role charity shops play in the business of recycling goods? If so, it would seem the members are against it. Or perhaps in their daily lives they're cognisant with the widespread, big-picture view that rampant consumerism, now driving the UK economy not quite fast enough, is ill-suited to the speed with which the finitely-resourced planet, on which in insupportable numbers we inharmoniously live, can recover from the consequential environmental degradation to which consumerism contributes. Maybe there was no point in trotting out such a view – heard it all before, thank you *Guardian* – in the committee room, small pictures on the wall. But, of course! – the committee had to come up with something new. That's what committees do. It must have been a relief to seize upon charity shops as sucking the life out of high street consumption. The resourcefulness of this analysis was what made me lift my head from my lunchtime preparations, better to get the drift of what I was startled to be hearing, and threaten with a knife the continued existence of a finger. But, to be very charitable, perhaps the committee's deeply secret interest is actually in the survival of the charitable organisations it has its reportedly mean eyes trained upon. For there's no denying that if high street consumption takes a real knock – less money about or a change in attitudes towards consumption – it will be the charity shops that will be first to be short of good stock. Good enough that is, in my eyes, for a classy actress to show off.

# ON ONLY CHILDREN

He or she is an only child. When someone is referred to in this way, the implication is that such a person is less fortunate than another who can lay claim to having one or more siblings around for company, the challenges that face this more highly populated kind of household forgotten altogether. Only. It is not rated as one of the more cheerful adjectives. When I have accurately described myself as such in answer to a question, I am endeavouring to make a statement without implications – state a fact of life.

It's a fact that one child is below average for a household. I first became forcefully aware of this when friends I made at prep school, an all boys school, started to invite me to their houses. There would invariably be a sibling around. If it were a younger brother, protracted negotiations would have to be entered into to stop him from hanging around, interfering, and generally ruining the afternoon. An older brother was better because in all likelihood he would treat us with the disdain we deserved, after some initial taunting, and concentrate on his more mature pursuits. A sister, especially a slightly older and pretty sister was another matter altogether and if it had been possible to say so without complete loss of face, I would have suggested she be invited to join us in our game of marbles, or if that didn't suit, might she have any ideas of her own for filling in the afternoon. I cannot remember a time when I didn't like the company of girls in a world where the majority of people were boys in shorts who didn't yet talk about the opposite sex. Making a new friend meant, almost invariably, entering into and being involved in a rich social situation.

My friends were collectors and liked swapping coins or stamps but not, I think, on the same scale as I did. An only child has a lot of time on his hands without sibling rivals to deal with, and during a snow-bound English winter – as they were during the 1950s – when it is dark well before dinner, much of the time must compulsorily be spent indoors. This was when I would make, organise or inspect my collections: stamps, tea-packet bird cards, autographs, soldiers, geological specimens, badges, birds' eggs, marbles, matchbox tops, model aircraft, coins (my father told me I was a numismatist) and so on. I still have some of them stored away though not, an eventual embarrassment, the plastic soldiers. This collecting didn't happen concurrently. One obsession would invariably follow another with a certain amount of doubling back to resume where I'd left off with, say, the badges. Collecting is still an imperative in my life, though markedly less central. One such collection, a direct descendent of a former one, is rocks of the world – a small specimen from each country or distinctive region I have visited. I hold the marble-streaked pebble taken from a beach on the Lesser Three Gorges, off the Yangtze River, and I am immediately transported back to the time before it was flooded – an igneous rock from Iceland and I feel the urge to shiver. A valuable collection with no swapping potential whatsoever.

No doubt there's a theory about why people collect things and which embraces the barmier reaches of the pursuit, spotting and recording the numbers on trains for instance – I confess I too was a trainspotter when my mother and I caught steam trains to visit her sister's family – and no doubt an obsessive desire to have absolute personal control over some matter comes into it, a hedge against chaos, a bulwark against death. But that for child collectors wouldn't take into account the designs of their parents, especially of those with one child who knew, against the odds, they'd got to keep him pacified on wet days before television came along and jeopardised forever the enterprise of collecting. A plastic aircraft kit, for example a Lancaster bomber, had a great many parts and a challenging, time-consuming set of instructions to go with them. Equally, a job lot of a few hundred common stamps takes considerable time and concentration to sort into countries of origin – the hefty Stanley Gibbons book on hand to consult for valuations. I do not for a moment regret all of the sticking and assembling, the sorting and affixing – it was utterly absorbing, the stamps with their exotic pictures were a source of wonder: miniature windows I possessed into other worlds that possessed me. With these collections, rather than, for example, the matchbox tops, my parents were on a winner and surely knew the benefits, in my early years, of keeping the affordable necessities coming my way.

One collection I began got off to a very bad start, although at the time I didn't realise it *was* the beginning of a collection – one to which I would maintain a lifetime commitment. Its genesis reinforced the fact that I had a major flaw in my character. I had submitted an item to the monthly readers' jokes prize of a comic to which I subscribed – and therefore collected – and, to my astonishment and pride, it was published with an accompanying cartoon. I can't remember what this laugh was, indeed I've never been good at memorizing jokes and have a repertoire of about five to select from should the occasion require one. What I do remember is that I was rewarded with ten shillings as the prize. I promptly cashed the order and set off for the local Northwood Hills hi-fi and record shop. We were at a transition stage at the time – I must have been about nine – 78s giving way to 45s, and I re-entered the street with three secondhand 78s. We had a radiogram at home, a heavy piece of furniture with dark green velvet on the turntable, which was nearly always dormant; but I was about to change that. Too shy in the shop to ask to hear the records first, I'd bought them on spec and hoped for the best. At home, it quickly became clear, to my ear at any rate, that two of them were duds and the third, a jazzy number about fish which contained a good deal of scat, was pretty good. I've since tried to track it down but no amount of googling on the internet has provided me with any clue about the identity of the artist and name of the tune, gone the way of most 78s into oblivion. I was cross-examined by my parents about the racket now that we'd suddenly become a musical household. It must have been a Saturday since both were at home. It quickly became clear that I'd have to edge away from my father – when in severe trouble I could never get much further than the front gate before he grabbed me for a hiding – because he now had the high colour and tone of voice that accompanied such an occasion. A brother, especially, or a sister, might have drawn off some of the heat and, indeed, made me less of what I then demonstrably was: selfish. 'You selfish boy!' I heard shouted, as I had heard it before and would hear it again. It's true, although I'd done the writing and posting and had thought of sending the joke, it was my father who had alerted me to its possibilities, and it was now the case that I had got carried away and squandered the good fortune on myself alone. Terrified, I quickly realised my mistake and regretted it, especially after I'd been confined to my room where, in a calmer though depressed frame of mind, I realised again that, for all this trouble, two of the records were worthless duds and I would have been just as well off and, better, unselfish if I'd given each member of the family a third of the winnings and bought only the fish song.

This unfortunate beginning didn't put me off gradually building a modest collection of records, putting in requests far and wide on the approach of a birthday or at Christmas. I don't think my parents liked my favourite record of the three – perhaps this contributed to the excitement – or my first 45, 'My Old Man's a Dustman' by Lonnie Donegan which was really the beginning of concentrated listening – the radiogram by then upgraded to a hi-fi after successful lobbying. I still have a copy of the 45. It's a classic. My younger daughter, especially, used to frequently play it, still cheerful more than thirty years later. Music: it was clear to me that it elicited total immersion and provided instant company, rhythm, a heartbeat. If there's a rock or pop trivia quiz question to be answered, look no further than someone who was an only child for the answer.

Eventually, I would have occasion to visit for some months a country where selfish, only children, a few of them, are born to rule: China. One child. It's a policy I'm qualified to comment upon. Think of it: millions of people, a generation, with a higher degree than normal of self-absorption, all reaching maturity and needing to co-operate in society. Each child, in an increasingly competitive and middle-class country, the focus of family pressure to succeed for its future security – there won't be a lot of time to listen to CDs. Only one child on whom to practice parenting and make – forgivable – mistakes. This should be my kind of country. It was, but for other reasons. I would see families in parks taking their one child for an outing, be invited to visit for a meal a small high-rise apartment and meet the boy or girl upon whom the future depended and see that here the word 'only' as applied to children and used in a comparative way has no meaning. They will never have the opportunity, as I have recently had, to make a quick analysis of the varying backgrounds of their friends and lovers, past and present, and discover that, with two exceptions in my case – women, mirrors for a while from which only-ness lovingly looked back – those who were only children barely feature. In fact a striking number come from large, generous families where there was, of necessity not policy, a lot of sharing to be done – and much to be said during dinner, all of the family gathered, in the way a much larger number of families once did. The conclusion I have reached, with regard to my fellow issue from brother and sister free families, is that I shelter instinctive reservations about us.

# ON BIRDWATCHING

I have recently taken up birdwatching. This doesn't mean that all of my life I've ignored birds. On the contrary. Birds or, as your aloof ornithologist will call them, avifauna, have always been a focus of my attention. As a boy, I stole their eggs for my collection, having been shown how to 'blow' them – just one from a blackbird's, wren's or robin's nest, out of the question now. The blue tits' eggs in the bird box fixed to our garage wall were off limits because, it seems reasonable to suggest, wild nests were fair game but not the eggs of a bird you had lured into the domestic realm by providing classy accommodation. Anyway, the box was rather high – we had a cat named Sam – and I contented myself with watching the little blue-capped birds flit in and out of the hole with wonderful agility and speed. So I knew something about the behaviour of birds from an early age – that a magpie could see off a jay, for instance.

The reason I have now, at a particular date, many years later, my eyesight not quite what it was – more of this shortly – accorded myself the title of birdwatcher is that I have purchased a pair of binoculars. I have equipment. This singular act I have been vaguely considering for a long time. The urge finally won. Nothing flash – not the bulky sort with a leather strap which abrades the neck of a watcher of avifauna. Mine are pocket-size, did little damage to my wallet, which means the investment of my resources hasn't led to a feeling of having made a burdensome commitment. There's another good side to their size as well: unlike the serious watcher who needs to make field notes to boost his identity, I can go about incognito. For one thing that always worries people when they see a bloke with a set of binoculars is that he might have a habit of training them on the wrong obsession.

On the ladder of birdwatchers, I am on the first rung and have no ambition towards further ascent. It is a harmless activity, my motives are pure, and nothing more needs to be said in its defence except perhaps to answer the preposterous question, Haven't you got anything better to do? by saying it beats staying inside and watching videos or the news. It also demands self-discipline and study – no-one can pooh pooh these: self-discipline to get out there and do the watching and study to be abreast of one's guide to birds of the region. This volume further validates the status of the birdwatcher.

An essential point now should be made. There is a certain order of procedure. Firstly, you must locate via the wide and ever scanning vision of the eye, a bird. Secondly, you must swing the binoculars into action, focus, and thereby eliminate global irrelevance. In other words, it helps to be long-sighted. I am. But place the bird guide at a normal reading distance from my eyes, or any distance, and of late I can't read a thing. I can spot a darting wren hundreds of yards away but can locate nothing about its habits at a couple of feet. Reading glasses are, of course, the solution – I am all of a sudden amassing optical equipment – but they are a nuisance when you are out in the field. Birds don't hang about. And the fumbling to find the glasses would tend to make comic what any birdwatcher knows is a serious activity. Luckily, there are times when none of the usual paraphernalia is required and the rewards of watching and entering the realm of birds is just as good. Beneath a bridge, for instance, where on the girders sociable pigeons gather, and a click of the tongue or, necessarily, several – make sure no-one is around to see you behave like this – will make these underrated birds cock their grey heads and eye you with what can only be described as quizzical disregard.

# ON DISCOVERING HOW TO PROCEED

The writers are dead but their words live on. It's a clarifying pleasure to come across a passage in an author's work where it's clear that he, in the gender inclusive sense, is both the source and the beneficiary of good advice about how to proceed – self-reliance and wisdom neatly blended. Here's Charles Lamb from his *Essays of Elia*:

> Too frequent doses of original thinking from others, restrain what lesser portion of that faculty you may possess of your own. You get entangled in another man's mind, even as you lose yourself in another man's grounds. You are walking with a tall varlet, whose strides outpace yours to lassitude. The constant operation of such a potent agency would reduce me, I am convinced, to imbecility. You may derive your own thoughts from others; your way of thinking, the mould in which your thoughts are cast, must be your own.

Varlet! Now there's a word that belongs to another time and place. Even substituting 'rascal' wouldn't haul the passage within proximity of modern idiom in England or anywhere the English language has gone on to unbutton its shirt and loosen its belt or abandon its corsets – distant from a nineteenth-century Londoner's dutifully educated voice. The genial, charitable, insightful (we might nowadays say) Lamb, one of the Romantics, took his own good advice and would not be cowed by others – advice that a writer, now distant in time, might still judge to be sound (and Romantic) and with not a whiff of the earnest, professional guru we in the twenty-first century seem so often to need or choose wisely to flee. Lamb gave himself permission to think freely for himself, to go it alone. Any reader equally enamoured by the rhythm of the prose as by the general observation must surely agree that Lamb's essays are long overdue for a comeback in popularity.

A while ago, I was arrested by another piece of self-manufactured, self-administered advice, this time from Mark Twain, when I came across it quoted in a review of the lately published first instalment of his hefty autobiography, one hundred years after his death, as he wished: 'Start at no particular time in your life, wander at your free will all over your life, talk only about the thing that interests you for the moment, drop it the instant the interest threatens to pale.' Why, yes, I thought, responding to the plain, emphatic language of early twentieth-century America, having at the time repeatedly fallen asleep over the chronological account of an own life I'd been misadvised to read.

It would be an advantage to be weight-lifter when handling Twain's book (good training for the still-to-be-published superbooks 11 and 111) but, even when the volume of his non-fiction prose is turned up high so that there's no being shielded from – let alone falling asleep over – his torrent of opinions, Twain rarely fails to be entertaining. So I read it right through. Sure enough, he successfully took his own advice (Clemens to pseudonym Twain) and the reader never knows which part of the life and attendant thoughts he's going to parachute into next. It's disorientating and delightful. With this method the dull stretches of a life can be ignored, the tweaking of events (relating to affairs, subterfuges and the like) become unnecessary, and the imposition of a structure over the full catastrophe can be comfortably abandoned. There should be more of this kind of personal writing at full rev.

\*

Now I'm going to give myself some advice on the way to getting to the nub of this verbal excursion: get to the point and get to it as quickly as possible. To do so I must quote from a small circulation, struggling but brave Australian literary journal, *Famous Reporter*.

The editor, following a one-sided conversation I had with him in a pub, reported in an edited version the following account of an experience I had while living for a few months in Malta, specifically on the satellite island of Gozo. Australia was about to decide whether or not to become a republic. The day of the experience I outlined was scorching – pre-historically hot. I'd made a special trip by boat and bus to find the Australian High Commission in Ta'Xbiex, outside the capital, Valletta, having been told that the Commission keeps a range of the nation's daily papers for public perusal, like Australia House in London, the only ready source of distant news in the grim days before the arrival of the internet.

I couldn't find the right street and found myself in the shade of a portico, knocking at the door of the Egyptian Embassy to seek directions. Surely the folks there would know. But after my knock had been answered, and before I could make my enquiry specific, the man I addressed, smart in a suit and tie, rapidly ushered me into a small, gloomy room – or was it that my eyes had yet to adjust from the glare? – containing dark, heavy furniture, the sort of serious room that might be appropriate for an interrogation. I insisted that my business was not with the Egyptian Government, about which I knew little and cared about as much, but with counterpart staff from Australia. For whatever unnerving reason – we had a significant language problem – the now trebled-in-number members of the Egyptian Embassy staff, all well dressed, appeared gratified to have a prolonged reason to be on duty during the hiatus of the hot afternoon. They looked at me, I looked at them. Nobody budged. I insisted on my right to re-gain my freedom.

Eventually, interest in me having apparently subsided, I was back outside in the heat with one of the smooth fellows who cursorily pointed me in what I supposed must be the right direction. I don't recall whether I felt sorry to be such a disappointment to them; they had some colourful oleanders in their parched garden as a consolation. A short while later, along a dusty, pot-holed road, I spotted a limp – wilted – Australian flag hanging outside a building from a diagonal pole. The tall, iron gates, I was dismayed to discover, were padlocked. Through them, I could read a notice pinned onto the High Commission door: CLOSED ALL DAY FOR THE QUEEN'S BIRTHDAY. The heat of the day seemed to have increased.

Just then a small white van roared up, stopped, and shared a gust of dust. A springy Maltese guy jumped out, then looked expectantly at the sun-bleached building.

'It's closed,' I said, mournfully. 'You won't get in there.' The guy looked puzzled.

'It's closed,' I repeated, helpfully, 'because it's the Queen's bloody birthday.' I'm useless when it comes to hiding significant frustration. Malta, remember, is an ex-British colony, now a republic.

'Which Queen?' the guy asked.

'The Queen of England,' I said, unilaterally restricting the sphere of her influence. The guy clearly didn't get the reality of Australia's continuing allegiance. I pointed to the notice on the door.

Well, as it turned out, he was a florist, though the van didn't advertise the fact. Inside it there were a few bouquets on the occasion of the Queen's birthday, I supposed. The guy, unaffected by decorum appropriate for the day, began shouting loudly at the building which responded when the front door opened, seemingly of its own accord. A smartly dressed man – smart dress a necessity thereabouts even on a holiday – eventually appeared from the shadowy doorway and proceeded down the few steps to unlock the iron gate. He cheerfully admitted the florist holding his small riot of flowers. By this time, I'd mentioned my newspaper quest to him – goodness, there was soon to be an important referendum that must surely sort out such an unthinkable situation as this – and the florist kindly said he'd mention it.

I hung about in the sun, dehydrating, in my t-shirt and jeans. After several exchanges through the re-padlocked gate with a shadowy someone inside the doorway, it transpired that the High Commission only had the *Canberra Times* available, the most recent copy two months old. I declined the offer of having it passed to me through the gate after I'd been informed that the age of the paper was because the High Commissioner liked to read the newspapers himself first before offering them for general circulation. He must be a slow reader, I thought, or said loudly, I forget which. Then took myself off for what turned out to be a delicious late lunch, no courtesy spared by an attentive waiter.

Now to the point of this story, completed as briskly as possible since at about this time – to fill out the picture – I'd entered into a relationship with a woman who occasionally accused me of verbal digression, especially during breakfast when she hadn't surfaced from sleep as rapidly as I had. This by her account was not a fatal flaw and indeed only played a minor role in affecting increasingly sporadic worthwhile communication a few years later. But I digress. The point of this story does not concern, as I originally thought, my frosty relationship with the British monarchy, a limited matter, but rather, I now see, its real concern is more generally about how best to proceed in a really testing circumstance. This is what I supposed was going on in Australia – debate – in relation to its constitutional arrangements, something I would have thought the High Commissioner might at the time be taking a lively interest in, and a possible feature of the out-of-date editorials in the *Canberra Times*.

Tiny, conservative Malta with its plethora of saint's days marked by loud explosions of fireworks and the ensuing trails of smoke in the moonlit sky, had managed to work out the best way to proceed: having decided to throw off the yoke of the monarchy and become an adult republic, the head of state – the President – would be elected by a majority of parliamentary representatives. One evening I'd spotted the President chatting at a concert for chamber orchestra in the beautiful Rococo-style Manoel Theatre in Valletta. His incumbency didn't appear to be having belated explosive repercussions. So what was going on in far-off, silent Australia? No news had troubled daily life in Gozo – the much less densely populated island that provides both some of the fruit and vegetables for the mainland Maltese and, should they visit on weekends, a feeling of having escaped from a modern way of life visiting metropolitan tourists might find passé. Many of the fleet of buses, for example, hurtling along pot-holed roads in all directions from Valletta had then been in service since the nineteen-fifties or earlier with serious consequences for their suspension gear – nevertheless a refreshing way to proceed, shaking but very wide awake, to the Gozo ferry about an hour away, barring mishaps, from the central bus station.

\*

It might seem a comparatively easy matter for a writer, safe and sound in his study, to formulate and express what, for the purposes of his work, suits his temperament best. There, in his incumbency, it's as if he's in a safe electorate for life, responding to whatever demanding mental promptings keep him, like a responsible sitting member, ever busy at his desk. It's a big responsibility: who knows what's going to unexpectedly crop up next? He – a Lamb or Twain of this world – proceeds according to his own good counsel. As it happens, by accident or design, Lamb (in the right corner), was a citizen living in a monarchy, Twain in a republic (give him the left). The constitutional arrangements they lived under were being mysteriously, as far as I was concerned, debated in Australia and, I later discovered, it was pugilistically ugly. In the event, after the referendum, the sitting members of parliament would not be called upon to choose a head of state. The florist's business on the Queen's birthday in the Republic of Malta was safe. He, and only he, could proceed with a smile through the High Commission's iron gate – a gentle consolation.

\*

That's a funny way to proceed, we hear said, in mild disapproval, the speaker blithely aware of a better approach, and find ourselves readily giving the cliché an airing when in an unfamiliar culture people's behaviour contrasts remarkably with the inevitable rightness of our own. The fact that one of the reasons we've travelled is to get away from the conventions we adhere to, like a tired wardrobe of clothes, is forgotten. In the Republic of Ireland, or in any inviting country, the sensible way for visitors to proceed in the hope of displaying some practical travel competence is, away from the main roads, to be in possession of a detailed set of maps and not a crude giveaway version. But it's a lot more interesting – and risky – to ask for directions and, as it turns out, it's a better way to proceed.

Let me illustrate. A few years ago I was travelling by car with my companion west through County Cork. We were progressing nicely along narrow, winding lanes shaded by trees in full late Springtime leaf, when we happened upon a crossroads and commonplace quandary: we differed in our opinions about which way to proceed to our destination, in our reckoning still an hour or so distant. I was at the wheel of the hire-car but not wanting to test our mutual ability to deal with friction at this moment of crucial decision, conceded to my companion's opinion and turned the car right. Half an hour later I wasn't about to cheerfully say we were lost – the road had swung back to the east – but did suggest that we ask someone for directions. Outside a small general goods shop that serviced a small cluster of houses, a man of about eighty, flat cap on his head, shopping bag in one hand, was the first native we spotted.

A significant part of the afternoon had further elapsed before we made further headway. Having told this Irishman the whereabouts of our destination, he proceeded to provide picturesque directions in that melodic speech of the south – the soft consonants in league with the apparent ease and quiet of the village into which we'd brought our haste. He described features of the rural landscape, distinctive buildings such as churches, road conditions with special reference to bends and open stretches, T-junctions, telegraph poles and all manner of things, including historical asides and the dwellings of his relatives, which would indicate to us that we were making accurate progress towards our destination – and, to be sure, he said, not to turn left or right at this or that crossroads which would lead, so we would know we were off course, to another range of features lovingly described. A stream, bridge, another farmhouse.

Luckily, my companion was not the woman I referred to earlier who respectfully liked a man to get to the point – years had passed since then – so there was no manifestation of impatience when she whispered, 'Do you think we'll remember any of this?' I kept listening, hoping so – not having the heart to interrupt this man for whom the journey was clearly as important, no, more important than the prospective arrival at a destination with its room and a bed. Indeed, a fine way to proceed. Eventually, with many, many thanks, we left the Irishman behind who knew, at his great age, there is time aplenty for verbal peregrination and for us, somewhat younger, no time like the present to make haste.

It is worth relating one puzzling feature of that subsequently interesting but long and winding journey to Ballingeary which a decent map might have untangled. There is a small village – I forget its pretty name but we had to pass through it – that is infrequently signposted at crossroads. More significantly, as the weary traveller approaches it, she will recall that some miles back a signpost indicated that the village was four miles distant yet, now much closer to it, the next signpost says the distance is six. Thereabouts, paradoxically – and perhaps there was a less general Celtic lesson abstrusely on offer than I extracted – the closer one seems to get in proceeding to an objective, the further away one can sometimes be from actually achieving it. And yet travellers, blind to other options when night surely has fallen, must confidently proceed.

# ON AIRPORTS

A contemporary, largely western sleeper's dream: you are on a flight to somewhere, possibly on a jumbo jet, which is suddenly stricken. There's engine failure, fire or some such. Panic. The plane is falling toward the earth. The impact is beyond the nightmare, never happens as a psychological event, because the impending sense of horror has shaken you awake where, earlier, you comfortably lay down. The dreamer never dies in his dreams. This is the kind of dream that hangs around. Next day. Next time, maybe, you're at an airport, even though it's well known flying is safer than driving a car. Such dreams may contribute to the demeanour people often have as they troop onto planes. They look like the condemned.

Airport lounges are chocker with resigned-looking people. We get out of the airport bus or taxi with a bounce but resignation soon sets in. At major railway stations there's buzz, anticipation, a future. Atmosphere. People have picked up speed long before the ground-hugging long-distance train has and they look intent. At airports, even with an armful of duty-free, passengers look as if they'd rather sneak home.

There are two versions of this resignation: domestic and international. The former is a mild form, the latter chronic. In each case it is most fully developed in the departure lounge where there is no turning back. Mobile phone users know they are about to have an experience of severe disconnection. For others, the loss of control may focus – there must be a focus – on the bleak prospect of being served an in-flight meal.

Domestic resignation can be dealt with quickly, providing the smallish plane is on time and the queues at the check-in counter are short. The development of this resignation has a direct relationship to the size of the country in which the domestic airline operates and its efficiency. If you are flying Aeroflot, Vladivostok to Moscow, things don't look good. Aer Lingus, Dublin to Cork and the grave symptoms may be barely discernible.

On a different scale altogether is international resignation. It has the largest and ever-expanding terminals to itself, and let's not forget an important meaning of that word. Terminal: end. When we leave, say, Waterloo Station there's an implication that there are more stations to come, release from the city, but at Heathrow Terminals, 1,2,3 or 4 things get deathly slow.

Resignation as a condition may begin prior to reaching the airport in a traffic-jam but it really kicks in when you join the long queue that winds towards the international check-in counter. Everyone looks sullen, like prisoners lining up for laundry duty. The effort to get the bags to the conveyor-belt seems immense. First-time travellers should be counselled about the realities, though the profit-motive that drives the airline industry would no doubt prevent executives from countenancing this. There are, as all flyers know, three more queues to come before take-off. Firstly, the one in which shoes may eventually be checked for explosives – my own footwear experience. This is where the terrorists are weeded out. You may also be frisked, as in a police raid. I am in favour of this queue. Then it's the long haul to passport control where if on the departure card you have been foolish enough – as I was – on one occasion to scrawl in the Occupation box 'writer' you may be asked 'Of what?' by a uniformed person, friendly perhaps, though at the time the question seemed to me to be rather probing. That's the effect people in uniform have. Again, my own experience. If you have managed to meet these challenges – it's taken a long two hours – there is after a considerable elapsing of time in the departure lounge, possibly caused by a delayed or cancelled plane but this is not essential, the queue onto the plane itself in which a few passengers, inexperienced and insufficiently resigned, will think there's some advantage to be gained by jostling for first place.

It is the looming eternity of being trapped among strangers in cramped conditions which is at the root of international resignation. Sydney or Anchorage or Rio are all a long way away with barely a stop. It wasn't always like this. There was a time, in 1962 to be exact, when to fly from London to Sydney required the plane, a Boeing 707, to stop twelve times for refuelling. Rather in the way many people nowadays can go no significant distance without stopping for fast food to keep their spirits up. This meant the prospect of dropping into Zurich, Tehran or Karachi, for example, was ever-present, never far distant, and therefore the tension of anticipation was a constant companion. My own experience. What's more, back then, people dressed up for the trip – not as now when the experience of long-distance flying has become so commonplace that track-suits and runners are quite good enough. My mother wore a smart skirt suit complete with a brooch, stockings and navy blue shoes with medium height heels. The suit my father wore was a three-piece and, in the breast pocket, the upturned V of a white handkerchief peaked out. I'd had a haircut. We were emigrating to Melbourne, Australia. Furniture was on the high seas. There had been no preparation for this – a return flight to Paris for instance. Our holidays for the eleven years of my life had mostly been located in the 'quaint' little fishing villages of Britain. It's a fair thing to say, from my point of view at the time, we didn't have much idea what we were doing. For one thing, we were dressed for winter – snow. For another, this general state of affairs could surely be reversed. In short, there were no grounds for resignation.

 The plane, as scheduled, hit the tarmac at regular intervals. There was a lot of it about. I photographed my parents with my brownie-box standing on tarmac at stages along approximately a 180° curve of the planet – and as we progressed it got hotter and hotter. This had serious implications for our attire – the creases were an early casualty. These days, the approach is to somehow trick oneself into falling asleep in an upright position, knowing of the severe challenges to consciousness that lie ahead. Back then, in 1962, there were ever-pressing appointments with the major runways of the world and the sense, significant, of exotic places only a little out of reach. Something else that kept you alert, well, thoroughly occupied, was the interminable juddering of the plane as it sped along the runway towards a hoped-for lift-off – a somewhat unfair challenge to its component parts it seemed. Taking off today doesn't involve the same kind of personal commitment. Less edge, more resignation. Of course, I did fall asleep above various countries during the day and a half it took to get to our destination though can't recall the quality of my dreams, if there were any. When, finally, we arrived at our destination, I had absorbed sufficient experience for dreams of a wholly new and burgeoning breed.

# ON MY LASTING RELATIONSHIP WITH D.H. LAWRENCE

'What do you think of D.H.Lawrence?' This question was directed at me recently one afternoon by a young woman whom I've known for a number of years. We were in her mother's house – the house of my close mate – the three of us drinking tea and eating cake. There was a fourth visitor as well: the young woman's little daughter busy playing with toys on the lounge room floor. When the question was asked, seemingly unconnected to the preceding line of conversation, just the two of us remained at the table on which sat a potted anthurium, its perky crimson spathes doubling as receiving apparatus for whatever the sociable afternoon might reveal – in the way of a firmly authoritative male response.

The days when mention of DHL in conversation might generate heat were long gone by the time I first encountered his work. The trial relating to whether or not *Lady Chatterley's Lover* violated the United Kingdom's Obscene Publications Act of 1959 was entertainment for an earlier generation than mine – interested in the scandal not the substance. I was still in shorts. Given the explosion of sales following re-publication of the book after it was deemed not to be a threat to the fragile reading public, many of whom had in recent history confronted the atrocities of war, meant that in numerous households this Lawrence novel would be the only book written by him, sandwiched neatly between works by uncontroversial authors, daring to be read. Then, eventually, sent on its way with most of the rest to the church fete or charity shop: *Lady Chatterley's Lover* is not, unlike, say, *The Rainbow*, a masterpiece. A discriminating family member would surely wish to keep the latter on the bookshelf for the enrichment of future generations. And in relation to that fine book, it's now a long time since I've heard of it being rapturously recommended by anyone, young or old, who has just read it for the first time. Now, over tea and cake, my chance had come to encourage a bright young woman to do so. Could a member of a generation in her twenties, almost a century after *The Rainbow* was first published – then banned – still fall under the spell of DHL? What a question!

Her question is indicative of the eclipse Lawrence has suffered during the decades since I first read him, in my early twenties, when there were still disciples about, of both sexes, who were identified as Lawrentians. Who else would a curious young woman ask but an old guy like me – if so to her I cruelly seem – she knows reads books and therefore must surely have a few things to say about an author she's vaguely heard of (all is not lost!) but not yet been tempted to read. Curiously, since what essentially I was being asked was whether she should bother going to the trouble, when I think of D.H.Lawrence rather than, say, Henry James, I don't think of the sedentary act of reading, its quiet absorption. I think of physicality, vital encounters, the pleasures of the senses. OK, even the *life force* itself.

As a measure of my admiration for the man and his work, I could have included in my response to the question – and it was hard to resist! – the matter that over the past ten or so years I've made a point of visiting both the house where Lawrence was born and the *cimitière* where he was buried, as well as places where he and his wife, the formidable Frieda, lived during their restless, pan-continental quest to find a life, close to nature, away from the ghastly industrialised world. But if I'd engaged in such an excursion, the tea would have gone cold, and I'd have failed to make room in the conversation for the woman of the house when soon she returned to her seat at the table and, even worse, the small child on the floor would have had justifiable reason to scream, craving attention. So, those visited places were in that room off limits. I kept my response sibilantly in check: sensuality and its subordinate, sex; Lawrentian sensibility: the vividly expressed connections with flora and fauna. Did I apply to the work of that volatile, feverish man of heightened sensitivity, compliments of a tubercular constitution, the word 'visionary'? I forget, perhaps not, since I was keeping things in tight bounds. But I was also keen to avoid sounding preachy by getting rapidly worked-up about a personal enthusiasm and, therefore, quite possibly on my feet in front of an audience of one. I did, under the circumstances and being a foreigner to arduously thorough scholarship, neglect to mention DHL's propensity for showing via his fictional characters that men know better about what's good for women than women know themselves, source of an indisputably correct feminist objection to a slant in his work. Ok, the man had blind spots, don't we all, especially those members of our species with an inclination to preach either from a secular lectern or an elevated church pulpit. As I sat, facing my attentive and patient questioner, delivering my partial and biased response – I hardly needed her occasional prompting – I had still to reflect upon the fact that my reason for it being so was to emphasise the broad effect that Lawrence's fiction and poetry had on me as a young man: he woke me up. To read the varied works of D H Lawrence was to encounter in them the quest for the nature of being fully alive. Here, I finally said, concludes the lesson.

*

So, to the shrines – now that my response has been exposed for its shortcomings, the respondent revealed to be a bit slippery – where I've paid homage to the man. When I first began to read his work, I knew nothing about his impatient, peripatetic life or his stormy marriage. I suppose we burrow into the lives of writers or musicians or painters we admire to flesh out our understanding of the work, to try to fathom its mysterious source. One of the reasons we visit a shrine – for that is what the house where an artist lived may become – is to give thanks. In 1885 David Herbert Lawrence, the third and physically weakest of four children, was born in a cramped terrace house located in Victoria Street, Eastwood, near Nottingham, part of a mining community. There is no shortage of biographical material in which the house features in word and photograph such, in the past, has been the interest in Lawrence's furiously lived short life; yet none of this information will firmly dictate the nature of the experience a visitor will have – this I do now know – under its roof. Incidentally, Lawrence's sister, Ada, referred to it as 'the rotting roof of a miner's home'. It's clearly undergone repair, perhaps several times by now, for the rest of the house is still beneath it and in good shape – preserved for public admission.

To make ends meet, Lydia Lawrence, DHL's mother, had a small ground-floor shop selling cloth and its accoutrements. Presumably in the same section of the house where there is now a shop that sells memorabilia, to make ends meet today. I'd been taken to Victoria Street by a writer friend who I was visiting and who lived not far distant. This act of kindness had been bestowed on other middle-aged guests over recent years. I expect he didn't have to persuade them either. By now familiarity with the house had, I think, made him blasé about it though not, perhaps, towards the variously expressed enthusiasms of guests heading to Eastwood in his car. Squeezed by other terrace houses, 8a Victoria Street, conforming to the architecture of the town, row upon row, is best located by an expert.

It would be tough to arrive on a busy day, should Lawrence's popularity have lately returned. The rooms are small and few, modestly furnished in the manner of the late nineteenth century. The smoke from the fires, for cooking and heating in this and every other terrace house, must have been hell for Lawrence's lungs. Once nimbly getting past the memorabilia shop, the visitor has little space in which to range, so without much ado ascends the stairs to the upper storey and finds, through one door, he is in the room where the genius was conceived and born. There's a double-bed, made of iron, if I remember correctly. A dressing table. This I can clearly remember: alone and lingering in that dimly-lit room, I felt a tingling, electrical, at the back of my neck. Then, accompanying the sensation, I felt a presence about me – and knowing whose presence it must be, mentally, rather than vocally, addressed him through the silence, since this seemed appropriate. Time again began to move when I'd concluded paying my respects. Then I, sceptical about such encounters, left the room, my eyes wet, descended the stairs whose passage now found me in a significantly altered state of mind from the way it was only, I suppose, minutes before. Did my friend, down below, notice – as we drove away? I didn't at the time wish to attempt to relate to him what had happened. To do so might debase it. He no doubt observed that I was unusually quiet – in contrast to earlier – and kindly left me to my ruminations. Perhaps others had also come away with nothing left to say.

Lawrence only remained in 8a till his family moved to another house in the neighbourhood, when he was two. So it's a wonder that his spirit managed to find its way back – and very kind and courteous for it to do so during my visit! Two years would prove to be a significantly lengthy residency in any one dwelling for the author of a dozen novels, numerous novellas and short stories, plays, masses of poems, travel books, books of essays and, when time began to weigh heavily during his short life, a gallery of controversial paintings. Oh, not to forget the furlongs of letters, now collected.

There's a house I've loitered near, one of an attractive group of houses next to Hampstead Heath, north-west of central London, called the Vale of Health. It has a blue plaque above the front door stating that D H Lawrence lived there in 1913 – a brisk walk with a specific destination, once I'd chanced upon it, through woods and from where during the past decade I've recurrently lived. It is there that he must have been conceiving the generational sweep and fecundity in perhaps his greatest novel, *The Rainbow*, published in 1915. But since he was in several other places that year, both in England and on the Continent, it's a bit of a stretch to anchor him there. Standing before the modest two-storey brick dwelling, of which I've found no mention in my admittedly incomplete reading, the most one can suppose is that, in a still tranquil though now upmarket neighbourhood, he was taking a modest breather.

How many plaques or the like exist, identifying places where Lawrence lived? This I know from my limited trackings down – time and money a restricting consideration – they're not always easy to spot. I'd been staying in the Maltese archipelago when I determined to catch a ferry from Valletta to Pozzallo, a port in southern Sicily, and then travel by rail to Taormina on the north-west coast. The Lawrences had lived there in the early 1920s. It was a two day journey – with an overnight stop in Catania – citrus groves stretching indefinite distances inland under a cloudless sky. The heat was impressive and the train slow, pausing here and there as if from exhaustion. Taormina felt cooler, elevated as it is on an ancient tongue of disgorged magma from visible Mount Etna and overlooking the shimmering, deep blue Mediterranean. A dramatic location, the attraction obvious. By sunset, having found an affordable family-run pensione, I was sitting on my balcony with a view of the distant, smoking volcano, the remainder of a bottle of chilled, home-made limoncello on the table before me, a welcoming gift – the *signor* and *signore* of the house both very friendly – feeling very satisfied, half drunk, with the progress of my quest.

Next morning I made for the tourist office. I had the name of the street where Lawrence and Frieda had lived but no map. Did he know, I asked the young employee on duty, the exact location of the villa – the Fontana Vecchia – where the famous couple lived? *Chi?* D H Lawrence, the author, I repeated. Significant time, about eighty years, had passed since his brief tenure in the town and clearly all memory of it was now buried as if under a flow of magma, books included. The villa was not in the twenty-first century a tourist attraction – other readers of the *autore inglese* had not, it seemed, been making recent enquiries. The employee handed me a map and pointed to the street – a worthwhile walk away through the escalating morning heat – then thought to quiz a fellow tourism expert, significantly older, who'd just arrived at the counter. The metaphorical ash and smoke obscuring the location of the villa began suddenly to clear. The older man knew of it, having more of a past to draw upon, described its location and said that the villa was now owned by an American who reputedly didn't take kindly to literary sight-seers. Did I resemble one in my much-travelled, all-weather hat?

Eventually, I found the villa – the pleasure of doing so heightened by the passing of time it took to conclude the search, the perambulatory foreplay. Just inside the padlocked gate lay an engraved marble tablet, skewed and weathered, at the bottom of a bank beside the entrance. Though it was partially obscured by vegetation, I could make out its message: D H LAWRENCE LIVED HERE 1920-1922. Knowledge, it seemed, that was becoming a secret. Looking up from the empty street, I could see that the square villa, set well back in a wildly thriving garden of vines and trees, must have a wonderful view of both Etna and the sea. What a fortunate place to live! The air was heavy with scent. No evidence of the mean American in residence that day because, as I stood there in contemplation, I saw two diaphanous figures walk out onto the elevated terrazzo, the thin, intense man with a beard and the voluptuous woman in a wide-brimmed hat who both, with slow stateliness, then proceeded to fade completely, as if absorbed by the noonday heat. As hot a day perhaps as the one when the snake appeared in the grounds of the Fontana Vecchia, inspiring the Lawrence poem which begins:

> A snake came to my water-trough
> On a hot, hot day, and I in pyjamas for the heat,
> To drink there.
>
> In the deep, strange-scented shade of the great dark carob tree
> I came down the steps with my pitcher
> And must wait, must stand and wait, for there he was at the
>   trough before me.
> He reached down from a fissure in the earth-wall in the gloom
> And trailed his yellow-brown slackness soft-bellied down,
>   over the edge of the stone trough

And rested his throat upon the stone bottom
And when the water had dripped from the tap, in a small clearness
He sipped with his straight mouth
Softly drank through his straight gums, into his slack long body,
Silently.

My trance-like state, compliments perhaps of the after effects under a punishing sun of the previous evening's intake of limoncello, was soon followed by a desire for a decent lunch – a memorable *spaghetti con le vongole* in the event – during which I directed some rational thought towards matters paranormal and came up with the foregoing brief, provisional and weak excuse for the latest. I hadn't had such an immediate, solitary opportunity in Nottingham, well out of the vicinity of poisonous snakes, and thoughts thereof, and in particular the one at the water-trough Lawrence goes on to attack with a log, to his considerable shame, and misses, depicted in the entrancingly flexible, mimetic lines of the poem, written in Taormina and, finally, in praise of the reptile. I give thanks that this poem and many another from the same hand was not murdered slowly by dogged annotation on a first encounter in secondary school, such was the opportunity daily handed to our English teachers in classes of sleep-inducing tedium. 'Snake', real and symbolic, had by then silently entered many a room of potentially wide-eyed, impressionable students. But not mine.

There was no opportunity to 'see' the Lawrences again in Thirroul, New South Wales where, having arrived in Australia by ship, they pitched up in June 1922, a few months after quitting Taormina. No opportunity at Wyewurk, the name of the bungalow the Lawrences leased, for paranormal hi-jinks. The bungalow is hidden behind a high, white picket fence, shaded by trees, and looks rather gloomy under its low-tiled roof. No possibility, therefore, to spot an occupier past or present, embodied or disembodied. This may well be a frustration for a literary tourist who's gone to the trouble of locating the right address and taken a train, south from Sydney where he is staying, albeit a mere hour or so in duration. He, if he is typical, might think the current owners are at best indifferent to the high point in the history of their house. There's no plaque on the site to commemorate the matter – though further down the road on a small reserve, there's a metal one attached to a boulder.

Hardly worth the visit, he might think, especially if he took as truth Richard Aldington's observation that the Lawrences had unpacked their bags 'without troubling to see anything much of Australia but a suburb'. Aldington, a contemporary of D H Lawrence's, a friend who turned into an antagonist, makes this observation in his tetchy biography *Portrait of a Genius, But ... The Life of D H Lawrence*, published in 1950 by Heinemann. In fact, in 1922, Thirroul, located in a coal mining region, would have had more of the air of a settlement surrounded by bush than a suburb – the name Wyewurk a ready indication of the bungalow's frequent use as a means of escape, though not from home grown humour. In it Lawrence wrote at incredible speed the baggy, political novel *Kangaroo*, evidence in it alone of the inaccuracy of Aldington's dismissive observation. Lawrence quickly registered the moods of the bush and brilliantly captured them with an original eye, yet he wasn't in the least embarrassed to call his fictional bungalow in the novel Torestin – which at the time it manifestly wasn't.

If a reasonably informed visitor to the house was permitted to peek inside, he would surely discover that, windows open, one could hear the sound of the sea; below the bungalow, down a nearby steep path, there's a wide, rocky foreshore and evidence of the Carboniferous in coal seams lining the cliffs. By now, after my experiences in Eastwood and Taormina, I'd expected at least some kind of suitable event to distinguish my visit. I wasn't disappointed. It had happened soon after my arrival. After I'd left the train station, while walking past a sportsground on my way to the shy shrine – the surrounding houses *now*, sadly, looking trimly suburban – I witnessed a vicious attack. A small flock of white-backed magpies, well, a gang of them, a common antipodean species Lawrence would newly have spotted and noted, were assaulting one of their own.

Using their formidable beaks, they had it on its back, wings flapping helplessly, or, if briefly the bird managed to get upright, it staggered awkwardly away on the mown grass, before the attack was resumed. This species of magpie, which spends more time on the ground than most birds of flight, is fiercely territorial. There was no knowing, however, what misdemeanour this battered bird had committed – or what weakness made it vulnerable to magpie trouble. But, no doubt about it, the attackers were cowardly thugs and soon, standing back from them on the road, I'd had enough – stood in anthropomorphic judgement. Lawrence, I suddenly realised, might have been tempted to do the same – and later think better of it. I didn't have the inclination to hurl anything, a log, at them but simply approached the one-sided brawl on the edge of the sportsground. The birds quickly flew off, in irritated disarray, into some nearby flowering gum trees – the victim, remarkably, with them. I expect it was business-as-usual again on the sportsground – or elsewhere on their territory – after I'd ceased interfering with the natural order of things, and pressed on towards the object of my quest, Wyewurk.

Lawrence and Frieda lived there, battling with each other, for a mere three months before heading off to New Mexico, their final odyssey. By 1926 they'd be back again in Europe. By 2008 – the year of my visit – much had changed in the built environment of Thirroul since the couple left; they'd probably have found it unrecognisable. But what matter to the magpies the year and day (but not the site) of their notable brawl – similar antics are as likely to have repeatedly happened in any summer, to any number of witnesses, perhaps to one in 1922.

\*

Lawrence, I said to my questioner, woke me up. It was not as galvanic as an on-the-road-to-Damascas-style wake-up. I was simply attracted to Lawrence's vitality, the vividness of his fiction and poetry. He articulated a responsiveness to creatures (and to the natural world in general) which I'd not encountered before: bat, snake, kangaroo or mosquito. His prose was rhythmical – prose poetry – quick to celebrate the senses, the living flesh, sexuality. Life leapt from the pages wherein men and women sought the deepest pleasures. Lawrence's excesses of opinion or his impatience could easily be forgiven, a small price for the richness of so much of the best of his work – and besides, in spite of the excesses, he was not without humour. It has been said that he is a writer for the young. I was living proof of that. But later, much later, it's apparent to me that spirited energy isn't necessarily inexorably extinguished – vitality hates to be vanquished – in spite of the appearance of the guy who now shows up daily in the mirror. I'm still grateful to Lawrence. Recently, I visited the *cimitiere* where in 1930 he was buried. He died young, aged forty-four.

Lawrence had moved with Frieda to Vence so he could, as recommended by his doctor who diagnosed the advanced state of his tuberculosis, enter a sanitorium at a decent altitude, away from the sea. Vence is inland from the Côte d'Azur in the south of France, an enjoyable, ascending bus ride from Nice where friends of mine have on a few occasions leant me their apartment in the original, old town – the opportunity, on my first visit, instantly presenting itself to visit Lawrence's final destination. When the Lawrences arrived, Vence must still have been a market town – in the square men now play boules in the shade of trees close to where the buses arrive. From there the walled cemetery is only a few streets away, much easier to locate than other sites Lawrence's name is attached to and that pilgrims endeavour to find.

But not the individual grave itself, among the many in rows on either side of gravel paths. The day I arrived was hot, the birds silent, and I was the only visitor present, wandering up and down. Eventually, I spotted a young bloke, weeding, who I assumed must be the caretaker. '*Excusez-moi, monsieur, où se trouve la tombe de D H Lawrence?*' My modest French had sprung to life among the marble graves but my search was suddenly at an end. I had forgotten, not having read a biography for ages, that Lawrence's body was exhumed in 1935, cremated, the ashes to be carried to New Mexico for internment in a shrine in Taos, where the Lawrences had lived. The conveyor of them, I've newly read – in Brenda Maddox's *D H Lawrence: Portrait of a Marriage* – was Angelo Ravagli, the Italian Captain who would become Frieda's husband but who, during Lawrence's final years, was her lover. The conveyance turned into a farce; the ashes may never have left France. I was told by the caretaker where I could find a memorial plaque.

It's at the end of a path, affixed to a north-facing wall. The marble plaque states simply that Lawrence died in the town, and the date. No Lawrentian symbol, no phoenix. Nevertheless, it was a tangible object to which I could offer my respects and focus my reflections. I thought to photograph it, prepared to do so, ready to take aim. Then my attention was diverted – a sleek, brown lizard ran out onto the path from a crack in some masonry, stopped, stone-still, took its bearings, then shot in a weaving motion between my parted feet. Ever now susceptible, I elected in my astonishment to see significance in the lizard's timely appearance. Lawrence wrote in his essay *Fantasia of the Unconscious*:

> How many dead souls, like swallows, twitter and breed thoughts and instincts under the thatch of my hair and the eaves of my forehead. I don't know. But I believe a good many. And I hope they have a good time. And I hope not too many are bats. I am sorry to say that I believe in the souls of the dead. I am almost ashamed to say that I believe the souls of the dead in some way re-enter and pervade the souls of the living; so that life is always the life of living creatures, and death is always our affair.

The lizard, in the instant of my full, eyes-lowered attention – the lizard, if you like, in my head – could not have been a more effective messenger, paranormality thereby regained. I pondered this, took my picture and, soon, my leave.

Half an hour later, I was back. On the strip of ground a few feet beneath the plaque there lay a small bunch of dried, wild flowers, placed it might have been weeks ago. While heading to the town centre, sensing some inadequacy in my visit to the cemetery, I decided to buy a plant, and soon found a florist, offering a small selection of plants in pots. The ground where the flowers had lain was resistant, dry and hard – but the lavender, watered from a nearby tap, was at least another vital sign that a remarkable life had not been forgotten, unpromising as the plant's chances of survival then seemed. The caretaker, when I found him, agreed to include its care in his quiet duties.

During a later visit to Nice, I returned to check, this time in the company of the mother of the young woman who has recently asked me what I think of D H Lawrence. She'd not been made privy to the fact that her parent, lively and light of heart, brightly dressed, had chosen a potted rosemary, the resilient plant for remembrance, to go where the perennial I'd planted was no longer – a green memory for me but not, I unkindly surmised, for the caretaker, if there among the graves he still cared. The young woman's mother was new to my DHL caper, and humoured me. We may never know if the rosemary has survived now that we're back in Australia. The visit on that day, hot once again, was not distinguished by the arrival of a presence or a swift messenger or any apt happening, mystical or distinct – too much horsing around in the graveyard, perhaps, and all because of the man about whom, after his death, Frieda wrote: 'What he had seen and felt and known he gave in his writing to his fellow men, the splendour of living, the hope of more and more life…' Quite so – and now with some application to a young rosemary plant, I hope.

# ON TAKING RISKS

So, she's a risk taker. The diners at the table in the restaurant were being casually divided by a friend of mine into those who take risks and those who prefer not to. A stark but even division, surprising perhaps because, remarkably, we had all chosen the same main dish: fish. She'd decided I too was among the risk takers. There was no probing diagnosis, no sense that one category might be better than the other. It was simply that, the subject of risk having cropped up in the conversation – I forget exactly why – my friend decided to declare her opinions. I imagine each of us briefly considered if we agreed with her, whether we said so or not.

No doubt the others also wondered what evidence she had so quickly taken into account before the matter lapsed, as wine glasses were replenished, and the conversation rushed on happily elsewhere. If it hadn't – and it's probably a good thing it did – I might have asked her what sorts of acts did she consider to be risky, forgetting for the moment that risk might be implicated fundamentally in the trajectory of any individual life. She would, I am sure, not have bothered mentioning obvious cases such as tight-rope walking, lion taming and sky diving – those acts that thrill crowds unified by their collective safety. Nor, perhaps, unprotected sex. I don't think, given the civilian company assembled around the table, she would have mentioned situations in war zones or, in that comfortable restaurant, hero-explorers. Violent crime, either.

I don't know what she would have said but will risk it and say it's likely the acts which she was then considering to be risky – what might have passed through her mind when she divided us – are those taken by people whom she deemed to be leading unworldly lives, any dabbling in risky assets such as shares hidden from view. She was, I guess, mainly thinking of the risks associated with leading the potentially penurious life of an artist or writer – a solo flight through space and time. It was not an expensive restaurant – nor, for that matter, was it particularly cheap.

Does a big decision, seen by others as being very risky, necessarily feel risky to an individual when, for internal or external reasons, it has to be taken? I'm thinking of a necessary decision with desired but no guaranteed consequences, including pure satisfaction, that one way or another will seriously affect the course of a life. Deterministically, it may seem. A person driven to be an artist, rather than some occupation financially and socially safer, may not see the risks others do. The risk might be in not pursuing the drive. On a daily basis it's nice to think we can choose to take risks, not have them forced upon us. My categorising friend is a painter and would, I assume, judge herself to be a risk taker each time she chooses to enter her studio, acts set in motion long ago when, in a safe but now abandoned occupation, she realised she could not risk do otherwise than pursue her real vocation, financially unrewarding as it's so far been.

This occasion somehow reminded me of the time I first met the poet Peter Porter, thirty-five years earlier, not far away from where we were dining, also in London. I mention him by name not only because I had to find it in the phone book but also because, as an expatriate Australian, his reputation inspired me to contact him when, as a puzzled young man who had returned to London, I felt the need to speak specifically to someone from my adopted country – the one chosen for me by my parents – and who was, as a bonus, a writer. Peter was visible, though he wondered how I, a complete stranger, had found him. I told him: the phone book. He made me feel worldly. By then I was in his Cleveland Square flat – where he would live till his death in 2010 – with a drink in my hand, following a ready invitation. We were in the kitchen.

I remember much of what Peter told me in an Australian accent uncompromised by the society in which he had by then been living for a quarter century. What did I say to him? I mostly forget. Stuff about my background, I guess, how I came to be in London, the fact that I planned to write – not, I recall, what I expected to say. I was having a young man's identity crisis relating to where I belonged. Peter was more open, exposed his feelings. He began to tell me about his wife's recent suicide, his daughters' – at school that day – loss of a mother. I must then have mentioned that I was not a stranger to suicide, my mother having succeeded in committing it when I was a boy. Perhaps this was what made me a companionable listener. As significantly I was in other respects a complete stranger, with no literary connections to speak of and therefore no avenues for gossip, to whom he could talk freely. I was moved and surprised by his candour – didn't know then that he was conceiving the poems that would appear in his most memorable and personally revealing collection, *The Cost of Seriousness*. He did show me the modest study in which they would be written. He also talked about, responding to my interest, his association with and take on Ted Hughes and Sylvia Plath – Plath's suicide no stranger to the direction the conversation had taken – poets who, by then, I'd read thoroughly in Australia. Suddenly, their presences were in the room, proximate, like electric shocks.

There was no expectation or plan that we would ever meet again, though we did, years later, to dine or drink in restaurants and pubs – especially the French House in Soho – both in London, my birthplace, and in Australia, where Peter began increasingly to return to and where I'd resolved to live, work and, with luck, write poetry. Aghast, fifteen years after our first meeting, I failed to secure for him an Emeritus Fellowship I, as a member of the Literature Board, had recommended the Australia Council should award him; failed to get the numbers in favour of an award that would have eased his financial position. I didn't foresee his eminence as a poet would have its detractors, see that risk. He was deeply wounded, thought he'd been brushed off as an expat and that I'd bungled the proposal he'd approved, set him up for a fall. His closely written letter from London saying these things arrived on a Christmas Eve. By the time I'd recovered, replied as comprehensively as I could, and he, I believe, had received clarifying information discreetly released from confidentiality by a senior source, another letter arrived. This one had many closely typed and amended pages. It was his personal guide to Rome – where for some months I was going – the recalled detail about the basilicas and works of art I should see, phenomenal; generous, too, given the valuable time it must have taken that self-deprecating man of my initial meeting to write it. Both letters reflected, and are of a piece with characteristics – the candour, the generosity – I first encountered on the day I turned up as a stranger at Peter Porter's door. When through it I departed later on that cold afternoon, it was in his company.

He was scheduled to record an item for the BBC. Both heading in the same direction, we set off and caught a tube train. Rush hour had yet to begin, our carriage was nearly empty but nevertheless we chose to stand rather than sit, between the automatic doors, and hold on to the handrails as we rattled along through the tunnel. I felt pleasantly dreamy after our drinks; the conversation easy, off in some fresh direction. The arrival at my station – I was getting off first – caught me by surprise. As the doors parted, I hurriedly said a thank you and goodbye. Now on the platform, I turned, thinking to wave. As I was about to do so, immediately before the sliding doors closed, Peter shouted, authoritatively, 'Don't forget to take risks!' I didn't. The train accelerated out of the station and disappeared under damp London.

# ON BEING IN THE COMPANY OF THE WRITER, GEOFF DEAN

i.m. G D

One fresh and sunny Tasmanian day, sometime in the mid-eighties, Geoff Dean and I sped from pre-mini rush-hour Hobart through wide-open country to Ouse District High School. There we were to spend the day talking to classes of students about books and writing. It was mostly a double act. I forget what encouraging things we had to say about fickle inspiration but when, at the end of the afternoon, we drove out of the school, Geoff at the wheel of his van, we reckoned we'd done more good than harm. In fact we felt satisfied with our performance and reception for which we both received a modest fee. This meant that when on the way back from regional isolation we drove through Hamilton, a small rural town with a pub, we were sufficiently flush to stop for a justified drink.

There was a pool table in the pub and it was pretty much a reflex action for both of us to set up the balls and chalk the cues. We had played together numerous times before. During our second game – we were usually fairly evenly matched – a couple of burly blokes walked in, bought Cascade beers and took a casual interest in the game being played by a pair of skinny strangers. From the way they proprietorially lounged about, it was clear that they were regulars. They decided to challenge us, doubles, and we cheerfully agreed – after all, it had been a cheerful day, talking and listening to the students, chatting in the van. Geoff and I won, rather too easily it subsequently seemed, but then things had gone well that day so why shouldn't they continue to do so? The locals, who were of few words though by now we knew each others' names, suggested we play thereafter for beers, the losers to pay for the shout. No problem this for us, though we were somewhat savvy about their ploy. We chalked our cues, ready to aim.

Pool is a strange game if you're not an expert and, indeed, perhaps if you are. Some days the balls, no matter how great the effort you make, refuse to drop into the pockets; other times they might shoot in with a fine inevitability and then you stand back, taller, raised cue in hand, impressed by your own astonishing brilliance, the wonderful mystery of it. The brawny blokes, good players by our standards as it turned out, were clearly surprised it was the latter experience that they were witness to during the next game. Geoff and I, as a team, could suddenly do no wrong. Our challengers became moody and bought a round of beers with obvious reluctance. If their confidence had been shaken this didn't extend to their joint view that what they had seen was a fluke: they were eager for a repeat challenge, they, the losers, to shoot first. They put in a lot of wasted effort; we more quickly sank the balls. So it was their moody shout once again, one of them slouching to the bar.

No one likes to be humiliated on their own patch, those big guys least of all. We played a few more games but with each game things got worse for our puzzled opponents who, having set us up for a fall, a night of beers paid for by a couple of innocents, acknowledged that their prowess had taken a beating, though they didn't put it that way. Maybe they had kids at the Ouse District High School and be fucked if they would ever tell them about the evening of their humiliating defeat. Their agony might have continued if Geoff and I hadn't had far more beer than we'd planned to drink and a long dark drive still ahead of us, headlights frightening the nocturnal wildlife of southern Tasmania. We farewelled the losers, with thanks for an enjoyable evening and, ignoring the possibility of performing a wheely in the cold car park, left our reputations to linger a while in the smoky Hamilton pub.

# ON MARRIAGE

For a few weeks now there has been an entry in my diary to remind me to attend a wedding. That Saturday is now free. I have just crossed the entry out. One or, I hope, both parties have thought better of it: a third party had the job of getting the message through. A headline with, as yet, no full report. This is a personal disappointment because wedding invitations don't often come my way. I mainly seem to knock around with the sorts of people who now shun the institution, or don't give it a thought – which is not to say I don't know and am not fond of married couples. I am. I'm not against marriage outright. Some of them are, I think, happy in the loose sense that word is used to describe people who have not felt the need to untie the knot. But then, you never really know, or want to, what goes on in someone's marriage.

When detail of that kind emerges, over a drink or two for instance, and possibly at great length, the frontline report makes for grim listening. A married person, after the fourth glass of wine, rarely if ever fesses up that, years on, loving kindness, stimulating conversation and great sex reign under the mortgaged roof. The story will take a different turn altogether and, one hopes, the children, privy to the looming bust-up headline will never, so to speak, have seriously to read on. My younger friends have pre-empted this situation. I'm not sure which requires greater courage: to marry or not to marry, given our needs. Either way, in these more enlightened times, the force of the law will, if necessary, be ready to spring into action if one of the warring parties has changed the locks in a tactical masterstroke and commandeered the assets. So, no wedding to attend, no champagne, no bountiful nosh, no speeches, in fact, possibly no hope. Unless an alternative route to a loving domestic destination has been decided upon. I hope so.

I wonder if there are marriage counsellors who have never fallen in love, never married – rather like priests who have to listen to all manner of things about which they have no personal acquaintance.

I myself have lived within the institution of marriage but am no authority. It happened this way – with little fanfare. A booking was made at the Hobart, Tasmania registry office and a witness pinned down. Although a weekday, it was quite a busy day for weddings though, luckily, we were able to get a slot near lunchtime on the day we required. This was a day when the witness and the other guest, my father, who lived interstate, could turn up. If this sounds like a mean, though roughly accurate, guest list I should explain: all the other relatives were a hemisphere away, not in Australia – my future wife and I had met in London – and we were new in town. The ceremony was followed by drinks in a pub, we newlyweds the centre of attention, conducted in a similar optimistic spirit towards the future when we raised a glass or two together in the same bar after our divorce. Our relationship was not restricted by legal documents. But I am getting ahead. In the car park, just prior to our entering the registry building, my father took me aside and said, with all of the casualness of someone offering a boiled sweet, 'Why are you bothering to get married?' I was unprepared for this question. It was a hammer blow. As it was, I think, some time later when, perhaps inappropriately – though truthfully –1 mentioned this query of my father's to my wife, one of the most honest and understanding people I have ever met and who was now pregnant.

The answer was actually that we were doing it for him and the aforementioned non-libertarian relatives who couldn't attend and didn't have the contraceptive pill in their day. It was, under the cheerful circumstances, an obligation, the done thing. We, after all the generations of marriages in our families, didn't want to go it alone, cause upset. Be shunned. All of a sudden, minutes prior to signing the marriage certificate, the sense we had of generational coercion appeared to be radically misplaced. It put me off my stride when going up the steps. But too late to say, 'Hey look, it appears out of the blue we can take an alternative route' which is what my friends may be considering now, the institution ever being reinforced by politicians, churchmen and other parties with a necessary interest in social order. Besides, those missing relatives who were, in an incorporeal way, present in large numbers, might hold an opposite view and let it be known. There is mercy in very small ceremonies.

My father's next brief words about the marriage were in the form of a statement – some years later. He was of the unswerving opinion that if a marriage ended it had failed. I could only give him half marks for this analysis – or not even that. Failed! I would express the view that an ended marriage or relationship had simply run its natural course. Unless there'd been, say, a death or disappearance. But for reasons that will become apparent I didn't say that. Clearly, in each other's eyes, neither of us was or ever would be an authority on the matter. Such a person was not in the same room as us. There is professional training for marriage guidance but not, if you decide to go in for it, marriage itself. So there are a lot of people with the experience of marriage but few who can claim authority on the matter. However, if there's formative experience to be had it comes in twos: parents. Many a child would wish on occasion that a helpful person with authority, if their whereabouts were known, could step in and make sense of what was going on around them at home. I was such a one. Marriage failure was looming, if I'd known it, and its natural course had me stumped. That's how mysterious other people's marriages are, even close at hand, and the conduct of my parents' marriage even now.

If there is one piece of advice I would have given to my parents at the Anglican St John's Church, Hampstead, London in 1947 it would have been *Stop! Don't get married. Think again.* This might sound odd coming from the single issue of that marriage and with all the benefits of being alive, but then plenty of good inexpert advice is never taken. I have scrutinised the flagstones out of the front of St John's, stood where my parents stood in the wedding photographs and looked out, as they did, through the main gates – and through which they would that day pass into the afternoon. I did this with a real need to get some perspective. It would all end in tears for the groom, and worse for the bride, in a far away place, in 1962.

They were both good caring people if this is part of the definition of those who voted Liberal in the UK during the fifties (my mother) or Labour (my father). I was also for these parties. Both on my preferred side of the then mostly Conservative dominated electorate. These, on my vague understanding at the time, had a belief in social justice, concern for the underdog, almost wholly to themselves. I was concerned, more particularly, with the condition of my mother when I said to her in 1962, Beaumaris, Melbourne, 'Why are you so unhappy?' We were standing next to the polished oak sideboard that had recently followed us by ship to Australia. The answer from the woman whom I, aged eleven, naturally loved more than any other, was also a question: 'How do you know?' I knew the answer to that was beyond words and, like politics, complex so I just said 'I know'. I think she realised I was firm in this knowledge, worried too much about how it was affecting me, and this may have played a part in what was to come. I was firm in the way that I would find myself making a choice, based on all the available feeling and knowledge, about which parent to eventually side with, and cast a secret unalterable vote.

Some while after the question, weeks, my father and I went out looking for a puppy – the first pet we were to have in Australia. It was a Sunday, so it was window shopping at a pet shop I'd spotted from our new company-provided Holden car. When we got back I felt something was wrong. Or more wrong than usual. Recently, my mother had been found by the window-cleaner, collapsed in the garden. Another time she'd been to the cinema with my father, and vomited during the screening. I wasn't meant to be privy to all this but an only child has a lot of spare time to overhear things. For days, or longer, she would be lethargically quiet and then, behind the closed bedroom door, there'd be screaming. Home life was unpredictable. I was concentrating hard on my mother's condition and this no doubt contributed to the sense that my father seemed remote. As I would later find out, a lot of the behaviour I was witnessing was the product of being English and buttoned-up – my father a slave to good form. We didn't appear to get on particularly with Australians who in manner were very different to us. It was only later, much later, when I'd undertaken a serious investigation of this marriage, that I discovered my mother had become 'mentally ill' after I was born and been committed to a hospital. Or as my father would occasionally but concisely put it, she was 'mad'. But that's the kind of extreme, distorted thing a person will say after a few glasses of scotch when attempting to provide some insight into a failed marriage, and get himself off the hook.

It was mid afternoon. There was a chill in the air – our first Australian version of autumn. My mother had said before we left, not wanting to join us, that she needed an afternoon nap. So it was surprising to find her still up and about when we got back – and she said she was surprised we were back as early as we were. I noticed she was unsteady on her feet and wondered whether my father also noticed this. Soon she said that she'd take her nap. I was puzzled as the rest of the afternoon slowly passed – my father in his study, me loafing around – why she hadn't reappeared. What would we have for dinner? I crept into the master bedroom, as the estate agent had called it, and saw she was still asleep, lying on her side, right arm over her shoulder, at the edge of the bed. I knelt and looked at her serene face – said some quiet things. It was during this time, not long, though ever since it has seemed very long, that I realised she was no longer alive. I just knew. It was not only her pallor. Something else. She was utterly still and, unfathomably, absent. I didn't move for a while. Then with the self-possession which seems, necessarily, to accompany a crisis, I realised I'd have to rise, leave her, and announce what had happened to my father in his study.

He didn't believe me. Perhaps it was the self-possession. I had on occasion lied to cover my more adventurous tracks, and been found out – it was a severely punishable offence – but I was not equipped to make up a story that meant he no longer had a wife nor I a mother. Lying was an accusation he would continue to level at me too frequently, perhaps because in a subconscious way he remained angry that I'd appeared to take a senior role in this family catastrophe, taken control, initially, out of his hands. Certainly, when the police arrived, my first encounter with police in Australia, they believed my story. Or perhaps, more simply and charitably, he thought I'd made a misdiagnosis. I talked him round and he agreed to come and see for himself. A local GP arrived shortly afterwards. I was blocked from the room. By then the lights were on in the house.

It would be the police who, next day, would start the hunt for the suicide note – take the empty brown bottle of barbiturates as evidence. Though in my understanding a crime had been committed – mercifully, it is no longer – and decisions made in the light of a situation for which no one had been remotely prepared, including any version of the aforementioned experts, the atmosphere was coolly rational. My father was, after all, an actuary – a person who calculates, mathematically, life expectancy for the insurance industry. I don't think he ever saw the irony of this. Talented and hard working, he'd been appointed to an important executive position in Melbourne. A professional, even a marriage counsellor, may not bring the wisdom of work home. One decision made was that the nature of her death was not to be talked about – this decision was made unilaterally. We could, we both agreed, still have a dog. We would 'soldier on' in Australia, although I found out many years later, from the papers relating to the coronial enquiry that, in her note, my mother had said she was 'a failure' and wanted me to be looked after by her younger sister back in England. I think my mother had also behaved rationally and, clearly, worked out a strategy. She didn't want to be found by her husband dead in the marriage bed during the night. Nor, when she had the most – aching – time at her disposal, on a school day. This is consistent with her wanting to cause a minimum of distress. Her one miscalculation, I'm sure, was to think it would be her husband who would find her. But since it was also decided that it would be inappropriate for me, being too young, to attend the funeral – a funeral with one mourner in this far off country – and that I'd be better off at school, I might never have had the chance, finally, to see my mother. So, if it had been possible to realise this then, I would have been thankful for that, as I am, in a way, now.

My father was not a ladies' man, as people of his generation called certain men. In his remaining decades, there would be no other women, no marriage. He wasn't cut out for it. Though I'm not saying he didn't have normal, even considerable, longings. I think he did. No other responsive women came his way. He, a modestly paid professional without family assets, had entered the marriage contract at the age of thirty-five on the grounds, post-war – he had been in the Home Guard – of a wife being a necessary requirement and, when others might have gone somewhere to dance, he looked no further than the office. There sat my mother, lovely, aged thirty-seven, at a typewriter. She, the eldest sibling of four, who had been exhausted from caring for her – by then deceased – parents, was the only one not 'spoken for'. Recently, she'd had to part, painfully, from a married lover. Loneliness consumed her, and the widening prospect of more. For neither of them, just then, was there any alternative but to walk down the aisle.

# ON EMPLOYMENT

He works at Tower Bridge in the city of London. He operates the electro-hydraulic drive system which opens and closes the bascules between the bridge's towers when a large ship – higher when in the water than 28 feet, the height above the River Thames the bascules are when down – is about to pass through. The year is 2011. The bridge, as every tourist knows, is a landmark, close to the Tower of London. As you'd expect, for most of the time the bascules are closed and traffic flows across them. Motorized now, of course, but when the bridge was first opened towards the end of the nineteenth century, the vehicles were horse drawn. There can be no improvement on the other means of crossing the bridge – on foot. Occasionally, late at night, when the traffic is no longer flowing but has been reduced to perhaps a lone, straggling vehicle with headlights penetrating the slanting rain or a cold fog, a man or woman will walk onto the bridge with the aim, firm or fuzzy, of jumping into the tidal river below. Or it might be at the height of summer in bright moonlight. It is not part of the job description but whenever an isolate driven to suicide appears – his or her aim made apparent by the time of night and, presumably, by tell-tale signs about how they plan to overcome the protective railings, and leap – the operator of the electro-hydraulic drive system, who has a view of what is going on, quickly leaves his post, gets on to the thoroughfare, makes for the person, and tries to effect a change of heart. In this he has sometimes been successful, having stopped several citizens from drowning. Maybe sometimes he first phones the metropolitan police. Mostly, however, this shift work – an unusual job in a unique location – is accomplished without incident. An occasional ship passes through, the Thames no longer being the busy waterway it once was, and after eight hours of having his thoughts largely to himself, with an occasional break for conversation with a fellow operator – they may not be air traffic controllers but this is equally a job where an error, a lapse in attention, would be costly, and so requires a team to be on hand – he, at last, welcomes the next shift and then makes for home.

I asked whether I could visit him on the job sometime and have a look around. A night-time visit, he promised in reply, would be best – there would be fewer officials on site at that time needing to give permission. It seemed to me a surprisingly large number were required to effect the raising and lowering of the bascules a mere two or three times a day. The operator – I don't know the official name of his occupation – and I had met in a north London pub we both popped into regularly enough to eventually fall into conversation. It was there, well, actually outside in the beer garden with other smokers, that he told me about his unlikely job. Confided in me, I should say, since he wasn't keen for it to be widely broadcast, given that what he wanted to be recognised for was his work elsewhere, behind a Hasselblad camera. I knew, from distant past work experience of my own, that these cameras are only used by serious photographers. Still! The bridge job, oddly, seemed to embarrass this softly spoken, polite single man of about forty, educated at a minor public school, from Cornwall. The necessary job, to support his photographic art, was beneath him. This supposition I made in a public house, known for its live music, and with a reputation for egalitarianism such that no regular in the pub would comment or care about the arrival at the bar of a rock star wearing a pair of expensive dark glasses any more than about the entrance of the local, denim-clad, thirsty window cleaner who had shown up without a pair. Or substitute such drinkers with a blonde supermodel and a hooker proud of her cleavage. Only a new, clueless drinker would be likely, noticing who'd arrived, to elbow his drinking mate and make a comment. This was the last place, therefore, to be sensitive about one's part-identity as a shift worker at Tower Bridge.

The bridge operator and I would subsequently run into each other on the street, chat briefly – him heading off somewhere with his Hasselblad in a leather bag – and again later be part of a group in the pub, pints in hand, and ritually return to matters of mutual interest – engage in those sorts of conversations in which, over time once their boundaries have been understood and settled, it's easiest not to test them and possibly break a kind of shared identity that elsewhere, without the society of drink, might not exist. I didn't let him forget his promise, which he'd readily refresh, but as the months went by without the promised action, and I was soon to leave the country, I let my hope for a personal guided tour at night of Tower Bridge and its workings fade, though I now knew a good deal about them from within the pub. But not if all I heard was the plain, unlubricated truth. This I am sure of: if I had been looking for a job – as I was – when I was also about forty and living in London – which I wasn't – the possibility of having a part in the raising and lowering of Tower Bridge's massive bascules two or three times a day – surely an interesting job-in-prospect if ever there was one – and cheerily waving to a grateful passing ship's crew (these matters clearly within the job description) would have found me eschewing alcoholic drink for days in preparation for an interview should I have been lucky enough to be allotted one. After a record-breaking decade in a single job in my thirties, alongside other work, as a quarterly magazine editor, where could I have better retreated from exposure on the literary front line than into the secret realms of Tower Bridge?

\*

I am the son of a man who pursued one occupation in the same company all of his working life. That the company he worked for in the city of London merged with a larger, global one, left him unruffled. After he'd retired from the Melbourne branch, he'd proudly tell me that he'd only been absent from work for one day during his forty-four year career. My father was an actuary, specialising in life insurance – upon his mathematical skills the Life Department of his company was indebted for setting the cost of policy premiums. The day of his absence, in 1962, was the day of his wife's funeral. My mother, after six months in Australia, had taken her own life. By then, both of his parents were dead, so was his brother, mortally wounded in Libya by gunfire from a German Stuka in 1942. The one constant in his life was his professional occupation.

By the time I left school, aged seventeen, in 1968, the thought of embarking on a single life-long career filled me with terror. I visualised the desk – not unlike my father's in his Life Department – I'd be required to sit at, day after day, month after interminable month, year after year: a life sentence. Yet I can confidently say that my father loved his work; it commanded his interest. Some time after he died, in 1996, I was told a one-line joke I don't know that my father would have appreciated: people become actuaries when they find accounting too exciting. Had I known it earlier, I wouldn't have dreamt of unfairly lobbing it at my Dad. He had a lot of justifiable pride in his achievement – having risen to senior management level he was, at the end of his career, the boss of his Department in the Commercial Union of Australia, and Assistant General Manager to the whole company. I can only guess what motivated him – provided him with the necessary single-minded application.

My father was an isolated man: he had colleagues but rarely friends, companions on the golf course though the relationships barely developed off it. A psychologist might give a clinical name to a person with his prodigious mathematical skills, sometimes awkward and inappropriate social behaviour, and lack of ability to provide affection – cast him as a type. I am glad that I hadn't considered such a reductionist view while he was alive. Our relationship was often cool, sometimes hostile. When it wasn't, I'd try in conversation to dig into his past but could rarely get a handle on how I might proceed or, so it proved, get at the right productive angle. Even whisky barely softened the crust under which his personal history was buried. I wanted to understand him, get him – within reason – to explain himself to his one living relative; give me his take on things beyond the distractions of daily events. What might move him to tears? He didn't read fiction, listen to music, go to the movies. Just occasionally something would surface, a mere shard. Much was off limits, in particular an understanding of his deceased wife.

Communication must have been different on the job – interaction at a better, effective, professional level. My father's ability was evident early on, as a boy at Shoreham in Sussex, the boarding school to which he was sent. He'd tell me that he first matriculated when he was thirteen, too young to leave. What effect, lasting effect, did the experience of being sent when so young to an English boarding school have on him? If George Orwell's account of his own experience is anything to go by – Orwell was born nine years earlier than my father – it might have been a period in his life my father chose not to or couldn't bear to re-visit, even with the assistance of whisky. Then he entered the workforce – his parents could not afford to send their boys to university – a few years before the Great Depression. He studied for his actuarial exams at night. Soon the Second World War would begin. Unlike his brother, an accountant, my father held a reserved occupation. I possess photos of him dressed in the uniform of the Home Guard in London but never got a word out of him about what it was like to live through the Blitz. Still, by his account, he never missed a day in the city or wherever his department repaired to for safety – no prod from the Protestant work ethic necessary – and I believe this. Not even days to mourn the death of his brother or his parents – though surely he must have slipped out for the funerals – and I can vouch for the fact, after I was old enough to observe events unfolding in our household, he never once came down with a cold, unlike my mother and unlike me who caught them frequently. His office work, there in the Life Department, seemed to somehow immunise him from contagion. As the decades passed, J. G. Sant, as he neatly signed himself on documents, an actuary with a sound grip on the knowledge that he possessed the required temperament for his exacting profession also knew that the probability of catastrophe, personal or global, outside the strict routines which provided the regular income, was ever present – a boon for potentially charging, at a very rough estimate, through-the-roof premiums. I could eventually see, under the personal circumstances, no other job could beat being an actuary or better suit the man I tried to know and whose dedication to his profession was exemplary.

\*

I am standing in white overalls outside the sheds on the edge of the tarmac where the baggage trailers are parked. Stitched onto the right-hand breast of my overalls are the letters TAA: Trans Australia Airlines. This particular day, as I'm watching the passengers climb the mobile steps to enter a plane, I notice that one of them is my father in his dark business suit. I was expecting the possibility of spotting him about then because he'd told me over the phone that he was soon to be flying to Sydney to attend an actuarial conference. He was to fly TAA, the airline that I work for. He didn't see me loitering with the other baggage handlers employed on the morning shift, though he did know I had the job in 1971 of loading and unloading domestic passenger baggage and freight at Essendon, then Melbourne's main airport. But I wasn't about to dodge away from my shift mates and, perhaps, fruitlessly wave. Seeing my father climb aboard, I was proud of the fact that his professional standing meant that he was needed at conferences nationwide.

The airport job was the last in a series I worked at the time because, until I'd applied for it, none of the others had proved to be what I really required. The planes took off, my sights were low. I was still recovering from a psychological paralysis that had made me ill, severely anxious and depressed, the symptoms bundled for limited public consumption – that is, for a few sympathetic friends – under the capaciously all-embracing condition of my having suffered a nervous breakdown, though one or two more specific analyses were tried on for size in medical consulting rooms. It was easy, when nineteen, and with a suitable mental constitution, to have cracked up: you just needed to become disillusioned with studying for a Commerce degree at the University of Melbourne for which you'd won a scholarship; come thumpingly to ground after a surprisingly fast descent from the heights of a romance with a beautiful young and responsive woman who put Jean Shrimpton and Twiggy, the highly visible English fashion models of the day, in the shade; discover and read *The Outsider* by Albert Camus and follow this up by developing a personal affinity with Edvard Munch's painting 'The Scream'; and then, after a session or two with a psychiatrist, who will soon want to knock you senseless with prescription drugs, the list of causes will extend impressively with particular emphasis on parents, the living father and the long-dead mother and then, to add some pre-pubescent, erotic colour, implicate your school French teacher, who having taken certain taboo liberties, judiciously fled across the Tasman to some remote town in New Zealand. Nothing, actually, I hadn't worked out for myself – but that doesn't necessary place me on the road back to health. Finding where that might begin is the hard part. As soon as I was able, after hitting upon some cunning strategies to outwit disabling panic attacks – we remained for some time about evenly matched – I wanted a job, a steadying routine, money.

It's a credit to the Australian economy of the day that during any one month my father, the one occupation man, probably lost track of what position his son was managing to hold down – until the airport job – now that my stereo could no longer be heard booming through the closed doors of his house. I kept in touch now from a share house by phone. Drove a van for a lingerie manufacturer for a while – delivering locally-made products, those were the days! – took a break one morning to watch on TV in a shop window man's first landing on the moon at about the time of another memorable morning when, while I was sharply taking a corner, the side doors of the van flew open and two large baskets, on wheels, containing bras, corsets, the full women's undergarment experience, shot out onto the road – luckily quiet – eventually toppled, spreading their contents generously along two distinct trajectories to the considerable interest of the motorists who vigorously tooted. It was soon time to move on from that job. Several months at work in a darkroom as a photographer's assistant – I was flirting with following in the footsteps of my new photographer hero, Bill Brandt – was less nerve wracking than the driving but it was lonely work, day in, day out. I surfaced stinking of chemicals and it was, of course, eternally dark in the darkroom. So I lied my way into a job in a plant nursery – light! air! – by saying I'd left school early, this being a requirement made evident in the job ad, and potted many thousands of seedlings (I soon understood my employer's need to employ a boofhead, though I must have successfully appeared to be such in the job interview) and got sacked when the boss, a most assiduous sleuth, angry as well, became suspicious, and surprised me with a remarkably accurate account of my academic past. Anyway, I'd had it with the fucking seedlings.

I am now of an age when, at close range, I've been both witness to and participant in trying to address the travails of young men and women who are existentially stumped. They may be puzzled about why a beam of light which appears to shine so directly and clearly for others in the direction of a future vocation or necessary adventure for an advancement of learning, leaves them stalled, clench-fisted, in the dark. They've often had a gutful of formal education and, quite possibly, of their successful parents who want them to see their education through to the end: a university degree, a ticket to enter a bright career, if only it were that simple.

A good place to get things sorted out is at an airport, on the tarmac, an adrift young person kitted out in white overalls in what may well, I hope, no longer be a purely male domain. He or she may wonder, as I did, why they didn't think of it earlier: physical teamwork following half a day's training about how to accomplish heavy lifting without suffering major personal injury. Then it's one plane after another – a swarm during late afternoon and early morning rush hours – and baggage, in amazing quantities for simple human needs made complex, that must be loaded, tout de suite, into each departing plane's hold, a reverse procedure required for the planes freshly landed. This is the easy-to-get routine of the qualified baggage handler. It makes you fit and, therefore, your brain chemistry changes. It makes you thirsty. It creates camaraderie among the sweating gangs who in 1971, at Essendon airport, were made up of men of every physical type from numerous countries on the political map, a few that were soon to undergo upheaval. The handlers all had stories and most of them a jaunty sense of humour which made clocking-on to a shift a pleasure, not a chore, and clocking-off, occasionally, a sorrow. To me, it was a restorative place to better formulate, aided by the comfort of savings, what to do next: university again perhaps, unfinished business: an unexplored departmental corridor.

There were wise old timers and young transients – there was, I recall, no hierarchy, though on each shift there was a leading hand. Even a couple of the blokes who put more energy into shirking than working were affectionately humoured – most of the time. I told English Tony, nicknamed Pommy, here on a visa, and Sergio, a migrant from Italy – who had a young wife and child (I made a black and white portrait of the family after they'd heard I was an old hand in the darkroom) – that I had an urge to create. But what? I'd also tried ceramics; poems were becoming a firmer possibility since they didn't require all the goddamned equipment. I wanted to make something that might provide aesthetic pleasure, and exist, autonomously, beyond the personal vicissitudes of my life, though I forget how I phrased it. Sometime earlier I'd flipped through an anthology of modern poems in the Melbourne University Bookshop. Several immediately spoke to me, if that can be said of a reading experience where it was the verbal energy rather than any real comprehension that provided the amazing mental jolts – and, instantly, I thought, I can do that; but of course the notion was absurd since I couldn't possibly have had much of a clue about how to proceed. I still own that electrically-charged book.

Those guys were attentive listeners, great talkers, workmates as well as friends made during the course of a year within the sound of aeroplane engines winding up or winding down, our ear muffs on as we ran or grabbed a ride on the tractor-pulled trailers, all of us so often cheerful in all weathers, no Marxist workplace alienation in sight. We took turns to clamber into the cargo holds, crouched and hauled out the baggage or freight, the latter sometimes creating distress – a couple of times we had to lift onto a trailer the metal coffins of soldiers killed in Viet-Nam – or alarm: once we pushed open the door of a hold and heard, to our immediate right, what proved to be a lion cub, snarling, in a large wooden crate; through crudely secured wire mesh the lion stared boldly at us, trapped sure enough, but it wouldn't have taken much additional fury for it to have forced an escape. Leapt.

\*

Occupational hazard, worse than the sudden presence of a small, angry lion: you write novels, get them published, few readers buy them, they're remaindered – a trajectory you might have predicted. Not to be wholly defeated, and with boxes of books about the house daily reminding you of the state of your readership, you put them to good use and employ the lot as mulch in your garden. This was the memorable and, at the time, much talked about course of action the novelist Peter Mathers took and with what results I do not know. I'd met him one day during the three years I was studying for an Arts degree I was determined to complete – introduced by a former lover of his who happened to be in one of my tutorials, during the year, the second, when the value of the course started to fade for me. At the time, to keep myself solvent and mentally steady, I had a small gardening round. It was not my horticultural advice that got Mathers out of the house, away from his desk, distributing hardbacks about the garden. His advice to me, however, from long experience, was that I'd eventually tire of menial work – lose interest in testing my capabilities within its still to me very considerable and interesting range. He'd had too much experience of it by then, when all he wanted to do was hold his nerve during the long voyage into his next novel. It would still be many years before I could fess up and identify myself, during long-stemmed wineglass social occasions, as a teacher – to the complete satisfaction of a professionally-employed interrogator if I said it was in a high school; further queries were the response if I mentioned it was in a prison – and to my own relief at having a straightforward answer to questions about what I did.

'Jesus, what a great job!' I'd said to my forty-something drinking companion in the pub when he told me about his employment at Tower Bridge – a job at his age I wouldn't, I repeat, have scoffed at; time at the controls no doubt effectively spent considering stratagems for the next photography shoot. It's easy to imagine a lot of routine occupations it is superior to – think, say, roadsweeping – and not only in terms of its unique riverside location. Peter Mathers was right: by the time I was forty I wanted more of what the kind of job at Tower Bridge might offer, shelter, for one thing, and less, very much less of what employment, in the scorching heat, making mud bricks, provided in terms of satisfaction when I was a university graduate, aged twenty-five, whether or not a Bob Dylan or Neil Young song announced itself on the transistor radio, propped on a nearby tree-stump, and briefly made my day which offered neither work variety nor shade and at a slave wage that would scarcely allow me to buy a small amount of decent marijuana. The days of working with mud and shovel, and the subsequent keeping of an exact tally of my weekly bricks production were from the outset always numbered.

This was Australia and the summer heat was building. I was living in timbered Kinglake in a shared fibro shack we tenants called Kinglake Manor – my room sparsely furnished: an inherited double bed, a chair pushed into a table carrying a new portable Olivetti typewriter – a birthday gift from my father – and not much else. The walls were thin – my housemates could readily hear me tapping at the keys and there was little architectural impediment to the exertions of coupling lovers though no-one was uncool enough to complain. Musicians, artists, seekers of intangible truths came and went. The locals, that is, the established locals – potato farmers, for example, from the largely cleared west of the district, or the mechanic or storekeeper from what passed for the heart of the place at a crossroads in the east – liked the convenience of calling the long-haired young men and the airily clad young women who'd lately arrived, hippies and drop-outs. Still, what the place at that incendiary time of year needed, as a precaution for everyone, farmer and fortune-teller alike, were firefighters.

All that was necessary was to train some. Five locals were hired following swift interviews at the local branch of the Victorian Forestry Commission. In fact, I turned up one afternoon on spec – to see if any work happened to be available. We, a mixture of blokes who'd lived in Kinglake most of their lives dodging from one labouring job to another and others, well, two of us, distinguished by the shoulder length of our hair. Tree huggers, Johnny, a big-hearted, large-bellied, jovial fellow soon got around to calling us – back-to-nature types were soft targets. 'Andy, have you hugged any trees lately?' was a familiar greeting. Then I'd say something like, 'You'll have to keep an eye on me today, Johnny, I might feel the need.' So, there we were, a raggle-taggle team, possibly the only applicants for the jobs and, I think, an entertaining wonder to our well-organised, good-humoured boss when we arrived early each morning at his house – in various states of preparedness for work depending upon what each of us had been up to the night before – for him to drive us to where our muscle was next needed, one of our own cars in train depending upon whose bomb that day was most likely to make the distance.

This was usually to go to plant rows of saplings – *pinus radiata* – where bush had been cleared for the purpose of creating a fast-growing, birdless mono-forest for lumber, the land often steep; other days to build or repair the culverts running beneath the

Commission's unsealed roads. At all times, now that the fire season was reaching its height, we were expected to be prepared to do battle with indifferent nature.

The training for this responsibility took half a day. The chief weapon which would, so we were told, be complemented by water trucks, was a long-handled implement that served as both a rake and blade. One was handed to each of the trainees from various fire-prone districts on the occasion of our induction into a fire-fighting infantry. In eucalyptus forest we were to learn the 'step up method'. This involved a long row of men using the tool – now a blade, swivel it, next a rake deep in eucalyptus forest – to clear the yard width of vegetation in front of them, roots and all. After a designated time, about two minutes, someone in authority would shout 'step up!' which in fact meant stepping sideways, and the line would go on with the task of clearing the vegetation – hacking and raking – that remained before it, ever moving sideways through the hot forest. Until, presto, a long firebreak had been established. This seemed to us novices a woefully inadequate way of dealing with an approaching forest fire, possibly driven by a dangerously high wind. The paltry firebreak seemed no more than an invitation for a spark to exercise itself in the considerable company of others, then in unison leap energetically across it. So the sweating effort seemed doomed to be of little help to the communities we were expected to protect. No-one would care then or later to predict that with no matter what modern fire-fighting weaponry was on hand during a day of maximum fire danger, saving Kinglake would prove to be impossible.

The pub, as in any small Australian community, was its social heart: nearly everyone it seemed went there to fraternise at one time or another during the week. We bushworkers impatiently made for it at the end of each working day. There were no social barriers at the bar and, frequently, no restraint. Our boss, the morning after a drinking session, would regard his charges with what seemed to be a mixture kind dismay and fond surprise at their commitment to the job. At weekends there was live music, dancing in the pub. A home-grown blues/rock band wrote songs about the place. 'Living on the Mountain', an infectious thumper of a song, was a crowd favourite, the majority in the pub on their feet, all ages and backgrounds, except for the very senior who tolerantly sat it out. We didn't exactly live on a mountain since to get there was only a half-hour drive steadily climbing on an unsealed road from the farmlands below. On a clear day you could make out the distant Melbourne city skyline. The Kinglake community felt itself to be separate and unique. On one occasion in the pub I found myself in conversation with a brash newcomer who, he told me, had just bought a nearby block of land. 'What are your plans?' I asked. 'First,' he replied, 'I'm going to clear the land of trees so that I can see what I've bought.' It was a short conversation.

Alternate weekends, we firefighters were expected to keep away from the pub and stay at home – take turns to be on call in case of an outbreak of fire. If temperatures started to soar we followed orders. One Saturday, my boss appeared at the door of our fibro shack – bush setting, wombats roaming freely – and told me to quickly pack some gear for travel: we'd been called out not, as was more likely, to deal with a local bushfire – during the fire season we'd already doused a couple of small roadside flare-ups – but a monster conflagration in the distant north.

It took several very hot and enervating hours to drive to the Mallee, close to the Victoria/New South Wales border. Four guys in the landrover with, between us, the experience of dealing with the behaviour of careless smokers up for a drive in the bush, and which didn't require us to call on our afternoon's training in the 'step up method'. The exhausted men we saw on our arrival in the Mallee, lying or squatting at the side of the road, faces blackened, clothes dishevelled or ripped, looked like the survivors of a holocaust. We could see crimson flames moving eerily within the huge black plumes of smoke on the horizon. That, we supposed, was where we were to go – all that was required were orders on our radio transmitter which now and again produced some crackling static.

Five days later, loafing in or about our one-man tents or else, by then, more likely to be standing each other shouts in a local pub and playing pool, we were less expectant of such orders. Central command, it may well have crossed our minds, surely had quite enough to cope with without our dubious help – a mild rebuke to sensitive warriors such as us, the Kinglake unit, who had received recent official training in how to deal with a potentially terrifying summer event. Maybe word of the extent of our training had even got this far north. It might have been a disappointing time altogether – except that we were each being paid overtime and I'd calculated that by the end of the week I'd have made enough money after tax to purchase a return flight to London – had we not the next day been radioed and told to clear an area in the Little Desert for a helicopter to land. This would, at last, take us to what remained of the smouldering action. It doesn't take long to clear a few square meters of spinifex. The waiting for an airborne craft to land in it is another matter: there are only so many inquisitive dragon lizards, under a hot sun, that will command your attention. Some years later, I'd recall this day and period of my employment; they safely sparked two of my first poems to appear in print, though perhaps for reasons of pride I didn't incorporate in either of them the non-arrival of a helicopter. Kinglake, the pub, wives or their lovers would have the thwarted heroes back by the following evening – and with the next day off to recuperate.

Of the five of us, how many – all? – heard reports on the radio from a safe distance thirty-four years later, or witnessed the footage on TV, of the inferno of Black Saturday in the summer of 2009, its human and material loss; be unlikely therefore to put quickly out of our minds the aerial shots of the ash and embers and acrid smoke rising from blackened Kinglake. The pub, valiantly defended, was one of the few buildings to survive.

\*

In most people's minds, a definition of work, that is, work that occurs in the workplace, will include the notion that it is a useful activity, and most people take it seriously: social theorists, especially. Back in the seventies, when I was first taking it seriously, WORKERS UNITE posters were a common sight in the streets; they're still around but in fewer numbers. Marx is no longer a popular secular saviour. A non-Marxist workaholic, thinking about his condition in a moment of lazy reflection, will battle with the proposition that we should work to live not live to work. Yet consider how strongly we are identified with what we do – and think how many of our surnames since medieval times acknowledge this: Taylor, Smith, Cooper ... work, work, work, these sample identifiers among the well-known dozens readily available for use as monikers in the thirteenth century, and reminders for any slack natives of the day of what they were supposed to be committed to doing with vigour to prove their daily worth. If work accomplished is useful, it must be useful to someone: not like breaking rocks in a prison yard, which some jobs surely resemble. Dickens, in his depiction of the Circumlocution Office in *Little Dorrit*, made a good start – we still recognize it – in satirising the time-wasting red tape that besets bureaucracies: employee as cog in a machine that generates ever more self-serving activity to the considerable cost of anyone obliged to deal with it. So, not all useful work is effective work, even though it may be useful in so far as, for another employee, it generates yet more work.

My father wanted to be able to say to his golfing companions, should they inquire, what work his son performed – reply in the straightforward way they must have adopted when they first became acquainted with each other and said, in turn, lawyer, real estate agent, bank manager, actuary. He didn't want to entertain the idea that his son might be a layabout – an attribute that in former times might have stuck in some version as a surname, Idler perhaps, to be handed down over the centuries – though I think he had his suspicions. For the chaps at the golf club, a firm identity was associated with smart clothes worn in the pursuit of a useful and respectable occupation. A Marxist revolutionary might have had the guts to thumb his nose at the whole bourgeois catastrophe to which the golfers belonged but I, actually, would have liked to relieve my father of his problem. It dogged him. It's little wonder that in medieval Britain when a person's legal identity first required the formality of a patrilineal surname, a given or Christian name would attach itself readily to the bearer's occupation, if that pursuit outshone, say, a personal characteristic or the feature of a dwelling place; an active, male slacker would surely not be honoured with, say, the name Wheelwright. John the Ironmonger, William the Fuller, Ned the Brewer would presumably have stuck to their tasks much as Chaucer's miller, pardoner and clerk identifies the characters when, in turn, they tell their entertaining tales during the medieval pilgrimage to Canterbury in *The Canterbury Tales*. Did my father's golfing buddies, as they trudged week after week around the golf course, having exchanged a uniform business suit for uniform golfwear, share stories or yarns that somehow reflected their individual characters and occupations? Perhaps my father, who was engaged in a personal identity crisis on my behalf, appeared to the others and in his relationships with them – if ever he told them about his most recent week at the Commercial Union of Australia head office – the embodiment of what they perceived an actuary to be: methodical, a stickler for facts, wary of risk. Once he said to me, angrily, after I'd turned up late at his house for a visit: 'Who the hell do you think you are, boy, turning up at this hour?' That was a good question. He surely didn't know, and I was certainly stuck for an answer. Thereafter, I began to make a more concerted effort to give him fewer opportunities for such outbursts. He was no saint and neither was I – Sant, our Old French surname, might originally have had less to do with piety than with strong Gallic irony.

After I'd quit the Forestry Commission and flown to the UK on the strength of my firefighting earnings, I started to send him postcards from various canal-side locations. With the help of my crew – did I brag that I'd been made the captain of three? – I steered a pair of narrowboats, one linked to the other, along what those in the know call 'the cut', the variety of terms, specific to the work – factual matters – I used revealing to my father an advancement of learning, albeit feebly, in lieu of the emergence of a respectable personal occupation. I could have served him as should a true captain and guide towards an unusually curious passenger voyaging to a weekly destination in those nineteenth-century boats converted into twelve-cabin floating hotels – a welcome guest keen to learn the ropes and employ them to wrap around the bollards at the entrances to locks or at moorings, thereby to secure the boats. Each boat seventy feet long, sir, and seven feet wide, the motorless one in tow – named Saturn – is called the butty. The temperamental engine in the leading boat – Jupiter – is a Bollinger but, of course, originally narrow boats were hauled by horses walking along the tow path; the hulls of the boats low in the water due to the great weight of coal or clay or whatever cargo was on board – pre-rail transport for what we now know of as the Industrial Revolution. As we stand here on deck in high summer, you can imagine the hard lives the boat people endured, especially during winter; the families cramped in their cabins, the restless and hungry children's steam breath at sunrise and, in acknowledgement of the boats' slow progress, the ice constantly cracking at the prow if indeed the canals weren't frozen deep. A softer occupation, however, than being one of the thousands of navvies who in all weathers shovelled the hundreds of miles of canal into existence, dug and bricked the tunnels – you'll notice as we pass through the next one how continuously they drip water – the longest up to a mile in length, pitch black, once illuminated by candles. Just the thought of all that grinding effort is enough to awaken some guilty leisure-time hunger: the crew member on roster to produce lunch assures me, sir, it won't be long. But back to the facts: the stretch of water between the locks used for raising and lowering the boats – the locks shallow or deep depending on the gradient – is called a pound. A series of locks is called, more obviously, a staircase, and that's where the crew, and any willing guests, sir, can and do work up a sweat getting the boats through in good time. The gizmo used for opening and closing what are known as paddles, to admit or release water into or from the lock itself, is called a windlass. The brass arm, freshly polished, which I'm holding right now to steer this boat at a maximum authorised speed of four knots an hour along this fine stretch of the Grand Union Canal is, as I'm sure you already know, a tiller …

What I couldn't say to such a guest, standing beside me at the aft of the motorboat, was that I'd use this knowledge and experience to later write a poem – it now appears in anthologies – about the traditional way of life as it existed for the gypsy-like people who once lived and worked on the canals. The poem of no practical use whatsoever and in which there was no place for the small metal-hulled pleasure craft – our authentic vessels were made of oak – so in evidence during that and throughout any other summer. I might have mentioned in passing the name applied to those inferior forms of transport by canal enthusiasts and latter-day boatmen for whom the canal network had become a serious revivalist cultural preoccupation. Noddy boats were, by force of opposing size and tradition, expected to give way to juggernauts like ours. The knowledgeable owners and crews of the traditional narrowboats, some of whom lived on them permanently, were proud of their status, like members of an exclusive club – who, incidentally, would have found attending one of the golfing variety, for example, plain hard work – and with a mighty, constantly throbbing Bollinger engine to re-enforce the hierarchical situation as well as, for those at the stern, a pleasing view of the all-conquering wake that so often beached the hapless recreational noddy boats, along with their distressed amateur crews, in the shallow muddy water next to the banks of the canals, this was, all in all, a superior position from which a captain could write yet another closely-written postcard to a patriarch at his steady address in Australia.

# ON WALKING

The past is always a victim of the present. I remember that, as a family, we were walkers – especially on holiday. This is partly confirmed by the fact that when my mother, father and I were out in the country, one or all of us would sing 'The Happy Wanderer' – that is until another walker approached. We also had the necessary equipment, including a large grey rucksack my parents took turns to carry and a small brown one that stayed on my back. These were mainly to carry food but also maps, a compass (mine) and a first-aid kit. They were not casual walks. I can remember the boots my mother wore, brown, and over the tops of them she would fold thick woollen socks. I have no recollection of what kind of leather my father wore out or what child-size boots were compulsory for me. These will never make any purposeful entry into the present again. That information simply got left behind, memory jettisoned it. In respect of the considerable trouble we presumably went to in order to get the right equipment – I can't remember this either – and look the part, this seems unfair to the enterprise. But it's an example of how ruthlessly the present supplants the past, especially a relatively distant past, and there's no knowing how much is a victim of it.

This does, however, lighten the personal burden. One walk I do specifically remember was weighed down by all of the necessary attire and equipment we had at our disposal. We were going to make for a summit. Our holidays in England had always been, until then, coastal, the paths followed never far from the sea. So this walk was exceptional and I still recall with a private sigh the heavy demands it made.

We were on holiday in the Lake District, which incidentally, more than a decade later, I would from 12000 miles away re-visit via the poetry of William Wordsworth. I think we didn't know much or anything about him then. But like him, beneficiaries of the Industrial Revolution, we were recreational walkers and, on this occasion, in full kit. In addition to the usual gear, we were carrying thick protective clothing necessary for any climber on route to where the atmosphere is possibly rare. The weather forecast had been consulted and a map purchased and scrutinised. The target: Great Gable.

The length of this trek, long for me then but probably a pleasurable streak now, had been kept a secret, and for good reason. It was with some no doubt expressed annoyance I discovered, after the hike had already been well established, that another formidable Gable, Green Gable, lay in the way of the target one and so had to be conquered first. To add to this grievance, I had forgotten to load in my brownie-box camera with my equipment and this now means I now have no record of our achievement. That record is exclusively of the lowlands – several lakes, one photo of both my parents in woodland, and several of my mother near our hotel, standing, sitting or leaning, depending upon how I'd asked her to pose.

Green Gable seemed interminably long, disappointingly featureless, although, in compensation, the gradient wasn't steep. The final assault, up Great Gable, was where the serious challenge lay and, by the time we'd made our approach, I was keen to get it over and done with. There was no well-trodden path because this mountain is composed wholly of massive, irregular boulders – at least that's what we encountered from our side of it. This meant it was necessary to scramble and leap to get up it, try to keep the cuts and abrasions to a minimum, and in the process it was clear that our diverse abilities in these matters meant that we would not reach our goal in a tightly bunched family group in full song. There may be some more convenient way of getting there now, though I hope not. It would be a loss to the number of activities available for the development of character, which at the time was a significant adult concern. What I remember of our sojourn at the summit are the rewards of the clear view, the cairn and good picnic food, and being weighed down by the thought of having to go all the way back to our point of departure over the same ground. That part of the journey I, mercifully, forget.

Nowadays I love walking and cover as much ground as competing interests and obligations will allow. Our anatomies are made for it, and do not appreciate a lot of sitting around – evolution didn't prepare us for sedentary living. Long legs, proportionately among the longest in the business, are there to stride across a lot of territory – with intervening spurts of speed – in the service of survival, the rate of heartbeats per minute up, the heart fit for the task. I didn't own this positive view of walking for its own sake on the two Gables. Yet it was a walk with an objective, like the first walks of any significant distance I enjoyed.

An early objective was to get to and from my first school, Winscombe House, whose oldest pupils were seven. It was in Pinner, a mile from our house on the outskirts of Greater London. One of the enticing things about this journey was that to get to the school it was necessary to leave the main road and head down a long leafy lane with little or no traffic. There were woods to diverge into if there was time – grey squirrels to observe, green woodpeckers to be heard. It was quite possible to get lost in absorption – and indeed once I really did get lost and possibly worse, or so my mother thought. I was on my way home from school in torrential rain, cap sodden, raincoat not much better, when a severe outbreak of thunder and lightning occurred. The muddy River Pin, which I had to cross, had risen to the height of the bridge. I knew it was not a good idea to be exposed in these conditions, everything seemed in turmoil, which was frightening, and I decided to seek the shelter of a house. A pair of elderly ladies answered my knock on their door and must have been surprised to see such a soaked and diminutive pupil standing in their porch. I explained my situation and they invited me in. I was also invited to take off my raincoat. Then we entered a rather grand living room – their house was much larger than ours – very cosy with its comfortable, upholstered chairs, and before long I had a hot Ovaltine in my hand. I certainly felt safe here. We talked while we sipped our hot drinks and, before long, the storm had passed. I thanked the ladies for their hospitality, said I'd better be getting along, and set off on the rest of my journey home.

There was a police car outside our house, and a couple of uniformed policemen at our front door engaged in conversation with my mother. Together, the three of them spotted me at the front gate. It became apparent, though nothing very rational was going on, that my journey had taken longer than I'd thought, certainly in my mother's understanding, and that I was the subject of a police search, albeit small scale at this time. The River Pin was in flood. I might have been drowned. My mother was in tears – she was also, puzzlingly, very cross. I was hoping for a better reception after my ordeal – my father's response was still to come after he got home – though I could see that the police presence at our house was not something we would want to encourage. I was certainly not going to encourage them again now that I knew how easy it was to do so.

Another pleasure involving the walk to school was Anthea. We would either by arrangement or good fortune meet on the way and, all being well, get off the regular route. Anthea was fair, petite, seven years old, to my taste – and if we could get permission from our parents, we would also spend time together at her house or mine, even after we'd gone on to different prep schools. The school day meetings were secret and, without saying it, we knew it was best kept that way. Anthea liked me sufficiently, and I certainly did her, to let me take down her knickers and this, after my kit had dropped to my ankles, swiftly led to the mysterious pleasure that came from mutual exposure and stroking. We'd be off the path, in a field, especially if the grass was high. If not there, we'd be in the woods, concerned about being discovered, Anthea especially, which placed restrictions on our pleasures. But when she wasn't too worried, it was addictively exciting, which more than once made us late arrivals at school, possibly in high colour, certainly preoccupied, which is not a suitably receptive frame of mind to be in for a rudimentary spelling lesson. It was a longish walk to school, so any signs of dishevelment witnessed by the lady teachers would most certainly have been put down to the exertion of getting there, and the lateness, if necessary, easily explained away.

These were all walks with a purpose, an objective. An adult form I would eventually experience in Australia is the bushwalk, though I lacked the regular and well-equipped dedication to be able to describe myself as a bushwalker. This is certainly a good bi-pedal activity but it has a tendency, like golf, which Mark Twain correctly described 'as a good walk ruined', to be burdened by dogged purposefulness, especially in its purest form, which involves walking very long distances over several days, across hazardous terrain with a mountain of gear. Virtuous as this may be for city dwellers with an allegiance to the bush, its flaw is that it is a walk that sets out to prove a point, unnecessary for those living on the land who have to tackle the challenges of nature on a daily basis. Explorers, the most famous walkers of all, have taken this kind of trek to an extreme, engaged in heroics and, often with dire consequences, overestimated the distances required to allow suitable exercise for a sound pair of legs. Then there's that recent invention, power walking, whose objectives don't bear thinking about, except that not so long ago there had been no choice since a former Prime Minister of ours was a well-known daily practitioner, the Australian media straining to keep up, the walks' objectives having unknown repercussions for the daily state of the nation.

It is not necessary to go to any of these disciplined lengths to enjoy walking. It is not necessary to have any objective at all: South Pole, mountain peak, running of a nation, school. The thing I now settle for, anywhere, is a brisk walk for an hour or more purely for the rhythm of it, the spring in the balls of my feet and, after covering some distance, heart rate up a notch or two, endorphins on the loose, the mind imperceptibly retunes itself, pleasurably perceives, via the optic nerves, intentness on fellow human faces, wind expressed in the flowing of grass in a paddock and, with luck, no significant hazard or challenge in sight, ideas may declare themselves, freely transformative – or else, as if locating a familiar rhythm, memories may emerge of early excursions, and of other dimly remembered experiences, long held in store, now finding their way into the open, released into the abundant yet partial light of the present.

# ON TIME

If physicists specialising in sub-atomics confirm, in the wake of a recent tentative discovery, that there's a particle in the Universe that travels faster than the speed of light, we'll all have reason to feel a little shaken. For the cause of this, and effect, we'll be able to thank the neutrino. Since experiments suggest it might outpace the theoretically undefeatable light particle, the photon – absolute arbiter of time in Einstein's special theory of relativity – the fundamental principle of cause and effect will face a whopping challenge. If the pushy neutrino, zillions passing through and about all of us at this very moment, can indeed burrow back in time, from its mini-perspective the principle must seemingly be reversed – cause can follow effect. Impossible to comprehend and as amazing as if I discovered, cue in hand, the 'end' of a game of pool was in fact the 'beginning', the balls hopping out of the pockets, fleeing from the cues, to settle in the formal triangular configuration so important at the 'beginning' of a game, no-one now set to boast of being a winner. From that super-size perspective I can at least visualise the action, cinematically, the players scurrying idiotically backwards. But I don't really get it.

For a long time, if I can so put it, I've been partial to the theory that all time, past, present and future, is somehow contemporaneous – 'eternally present' as T S Eliot said. Consistently beyond comprehension, I would add, though it might explain why prophetic activity can be accurate. I once knew a man who dreamt about the winners of forthcoming horse races, presumably pre-cheering the horses across the finishing line – sure bets for a time. Then the gift deserted him and he was back to cursing losers, nursing financial hurt, till wisely he quit the addiction. Somehow as he lay supine beside his wife in the dark, the race meetings which were well into the future for thousands of others punters found him already next to the racetrack, via the main gate. Presumably in a loudly cheering crowd both there and yet to be there, insomniac or asleep – linear time thereby astonishingly given the slip. Or perhaps there's a better, less remarkable explanation, since prophecy is not the most respected of activities thanks to crazy doomsayers who give it a bad press, discredit it. In any case, I suppose dreaming of a few race winners seems a rather pathetic return for wild and accurate prophetic flight – and it didn't endure the test of time, whatever time is. More like an ocean than a rapid. Both.

Time is notably elastic, from a practical viewpoint – long in passing when you're in an immobilised queue or stuck at a duff dinner party, tight when late for a plane flight or trespassing for gain on the wrong side of the law. How strangely it passes! Time is defiantly pliable, depending on events, to its mocking advantage. When young we fall into historical time with a thud – without Herodotus or any guide to the past to hurriedly right us. By the time we stumble as if half-blind through sentences in stories and become blessed with a gift for unconventional spelling, we are sharply – lucidly – aware that there is a past, and before long a past tense, that is freighted with consequence. That past is startlingly, narcissistically our own: never more persuasively present, and such equilibrium as exists more thoroughly scuttled, when a childhood act is parentally judged to be trouble, no room in the house to hide from it. Trouble is glue. A decade or so later we may each have agreed, thanks to James Joyce, history is a nightmare from which we are trying to awake. The statement resonates as truth – just as we've always known that a schoolyard is a great place for a bruising. By then it may be, in effect, that we've vertically scaled the historical time-line we've been introduced to in class, starting in Bronze Age Mesopotamia, long effort expended in sizing up nations rising and falling – and since it's a detailed time-line we've seen, the designer's range of colours is stretched – to arrive thereafter breathlessly in the present, having clung all the way to necessary dates, the ones we've guessed are about to be tested. Now when exactly did the Battle of Thermopylae happen? I forget. For this I blame the cruel passage of time. Other battles I remember.

In our neighbourhood, in the fifties, contemporary strife when not caused by misdemeanours at home was all the work of the Germans. Given time, and fine weather, we kids were ready to kill some – placing a great deal of faith in plastic guns. There was an air-raid shelter nearby, bricked up, out of bounds. No matter. We had a dairy farm at hand where we could wage war, very loosely re-enact the battles of the recent past. A few of the boys' fathers were the farmers – and with the job came a tied cottage, a modern reminder of feudal times. Our semi-detached house was opposite. From the second storey bedroom window I could see the open fields, the barn, and milking sheds where we'd dodge invisible bullets. This was in outer London, the farm having survived suburban encroachment and the Luftwaffe. None of the neighbourhood had been bombed.

It was tough to play a German – tough thereabouts in modest houses to be a grown-up outer Londoner, in civvies, dealing with post-war austerity – war comics evidence that in the immediate circumstances our perceptions would be shaped by events in historical time, nothing greater. To play a German was to be, we little lads knew from our avid reading, on the side set to be routed, no matter how defiant the shrieking Stukas were in the skies or how many furious imperatives the enemy bellowed. But someone had to put their hand up – no-one wanted to be a Kraut and there weren't very many of us to go around, so if you'd previously had the honour of being British, it was gracious to volunteer. Then there was fast movement this way and that around the haystack, guns blazing – arguments about whether or not someone had been shot were in danger of turning fun violence into real violence. It's a wonder our parents were so ready to let us buy those cheap comics – and so many of them. We were barely aware of what the war had meant to our parents many of whom had lost close relatives, we with time stretching before us without a conceivable end, them only too familiar with its perils. The Second World War seemed in fact to be long before our time.

Now I'm older by a couple of decades than my parents then were – and have become increasingly relieved at the thought of the existence of geological or deep time and its ready implications. This interest has long been maturing. In fact it started when the convulsions located in swift historical time were still being played out in the neighbourhood farmyard – goodies versus baddies, a black and white matter, the drawings in the comics equally without colour or shade. Learning about events that exist in relation to one another in historical time, beginning with the inconceivably remote and misty dawn of civilisation – the sense of hope implied in the clichéd phrase freshly misplaced at the time – seemed to underpin, from where I dreamily sat at a desk or surveyed the scene from a window, an adequately comprehensive time scale for encapsulating all that once mattered. Until I was given a fossil.

It was discovered in Kent. One afternoon a diligent gardener was turning the soil in his vegetable plot, in preparation for the annual spring planting, when he spotted it. The gardener was my godfather and the fossil was of a sea urchin. These weren't an uncommon find in a region dominated by chalk from the Upper Cretaceous period, the relatively soft rock marine in origin, calcium carbonate from shells, I later learnt, though not from chalk articulated on a blackboard. In fact my godfather, a rather reserved and austere man in my recollection, had turned up fossils before and had a collection on display behind glass in the family home. So he was alert to the possibility of chancing upon others and could bear to part with a new find. I could see, when he generously gave it to me during a visit to London, that the impression of the urchin's shell was exceptionally fine and, now that I had the fossil in my warm palm, studied it in reverential wonder. It transpired that it had taken about eighty million years to arrive, thanks to tectonic uplift and a garden fork, at this destination – my right hand at the time was accustomed to trying to keep hold of small creatures eager to get free, pet mice, and newts from a nearby swamp. The urchin fossil asserted a firm presence, iron-heavy.

Commendably, my godfather followed up this gift with another, a book about palaeontology, which arrived on time for a birthday. On time! Always an issue. Late for school, late home – commonplace trouble with its hub located at our place. When it mattered, time always seemed in very short supply. Now as I immersed myself in the slow world of fossils, all the day-to-day urgency seemed a bit cock-eyed, or so I might have put it. Then there were the strange and wonderful words I discovered: Jurassic, Cretaceous, Triassic, Permian … words that suggested real heft – and depth. An eighty million years' long period called the Cretaceous – the time when Gondwanaland broke up and mass extinctions, including dinosaurs, reached a peak – had in my mind an aura, powerfully elemental, that the so recent Edwardian period, for example, plainly lacked, though I didn't have any special grudge against it.

The importance of Kings and Queens, their chronology and the wretched dates of the reigns that had to be memorised, subjected to tests, then were placed in perspective by the earth-shaking geological periods I now read about. In other words, the history teachers could shove their sodding dates – there was a lively vernacular used on the farm opposite our house, severely frowned upon both at school and at home – though I didn't have the courage of King Richard 1 to carry out the secret threat. My fossil had begun its permineralisation many millions of years before the bloody Wars of the Roses and that process was really something significant to think about while gazing out of the classroom window onto the sports field. My father, not to be completely trumped on the gift-giving front, bought me a geologist's pick, should we ever entertain the idea of visiting some fossil cliffs. Meantime, I could easily see it might have more destructive uses.

I still have the fossil, the book and the pick – and now many more fossils. Fossil enthusiasts soon get wind of any fossil site that exists in a region where they happen to be visiting or newly living – if indeed they can't simply pick samples out of the earth in their gardens. Like other collectors, they have a keen nose for where the best treasure is sure to be found. These days the site may be on the internet from which fossils can be cheaply ordered – the result, often, of increasingly vast numbers being discovered during ever more extensive mechanical quarrying, frequently in remote regions, and sold to dealers as a sideline. Somewhat easier and cheaper to shift and ship than tonnages of rock. This source of fossils, and the burgeoning trade, I was recently told about by a dealer close to the British Museum. He had a fossil ammonite as big as a car wheel in his dimly-lit shop. I left empty-handed. Why buy a fossil, possibly have it dropped into your letter box, when you can get out into the fresh air and find one?

Alone is best. Unless you are showing your children the ropes before they race in time towards adulthood and find better things to do. Alone, on a fossil cliff, the silence emanating from the rock, rock that millions and millions of years ago was soft sediment, epoch-deep, hardening under the pressure of the sea – the silence is inseparable from the passage of time illustrated by the cliff. It is, in short, profound. The same sort of experience may be had next to sedimentary strata exposed by a cutting for a road, should a break be required from making motorised haste.   It should be popular, this kind of hanging about – perhaps it is and in my own hurry I've missed the evidence. No equipment is required, no fancy mountaineering tackle, not even a pick when covetousness can be resisted and no acceptable souvenirs therefore need to be extracted. In the presence of a fossil cliff – I once lived within easy walking distance of a beauty in coastal Beaumaris, Victoria – or any uplift representing a geological epoch the earth's energies have seen fit to reveal, there is more than a hint of human insignificance allied to a sense how recently our species has made its hubristic appearance.

This I see as a comfort. There's a strong sense in such a place that the environmentally exhausted world in need of a rest from human rapacity and greed will eventually continue just fine without us. The Cretaceous Period, fashionable for its production of fossils, and the enduring of mass extinctions, proves this well enough. Life in some yet to be selected form went on: now sea-birds circle near the Period's limestone cliffs, and humans, with nothing better to do, scale them. I recommend a day out – or an hour or two if time is short – at some cliffs, preferably fossil-laden, alone or, if really necessary, in company ( providing the companions will leave their time-consuming technological gizmos at home) to anyone who

- Wants to get the urgencies of modern life into epochal perspective
- Or needs a harmless displacement activity with mental and physical benefits
- Or wants to eat a cut lunch in peace and meditate, say, on plate tectonics
- Or is on holiday nearby and finds the resort in which they are staying is as dreadful as they fear
- Or doesn't as yet claim Carpe Diem as a motto
- Or has a long unutilised geologist's pick and needs a good excuse to swing it
- Or who thinks Homo sapiens have the final, signed title deeds to the planet
- Or............................................................................
- Or............................................................................
- Or............................................................................

The list will benefit from timely addition. Later in the day, back home – or back at the awful resort – things will have moved on, the family argument having subsided, if that is what the lone excursioner needed to consign to history, along with her by now solicitous husband. The human race, dominating the lately-named Anthropocene Period (but who'll inform a future dominant species?), will still be around seeming, after those hours of deeply personal geological contemplation, in an alarming haste to get to or away from somewhere. But the corrective experience will soon subside, sheer necessity shaping the change, when the answer to an inevitable question, 'What time is it?' – say, youthfully casual in tone – happens to be, without any global implication, a parentally tired-of-waiting impatient 'It's getting late'.

# ON TRUST

On Bob Dylan's twenty-third official album, *Empire Burlesque*, there's a song called 'Trust Yourself' in which the refrain is: 'If you need somebody you can trust, trust yourself'. Dylan, a man who has attracted a lot of criticism – opprobrium – at various times in his long career, is entitled to remind himself, and us, of this point. Indeed, I recently read in *The New York Review of Books* that in the opinion of the writer of a tough article about Dylan, *Empire Burlesque* qualifies as the album that exists at the nadir of his career. I doubt now whether the observation would make Dylan remotely shift in his seat. Over the years he's come in for a good kicking from those who reckon they know better than he does about which direction his music should be taking. No doubt he's been both bemused and annoyed by this – and proceeded to trust his own judgement. It has paid off.

Trusting yourself is one thing. Trusting others quite another. On a daily basis we need basic trust to get by. This might apply to the plumbing, household security and endless other things we trust will serve us, until there's a hitch. Trust, it turns out, and as we hear said, often has to be earned, is not a given. Mostly. It is a form of capital. Politicians try rapidly to earn it, squander it as fast because the general public, ever hopeful but serially afflicted by mass amnesia, forget that politicians, like the rest of us, have or develop vested interests, and common failings. We become energised, at dinner parties, by our lack of trust in the political class – can regularly bank on it. Our innate, readily alerted suspicion of others is as attracted to highly visible politicians as our savings are to the highest interest-bearing accounts. Which is not to say we shouldn't expect better. We often do. So, I imagine, do many of our elected representatives when they, on their first day in parliament, are getting the feel of their seats on the backbenches.

Distrust, fairly or unfairly, has plenty of regular targets, finds swift dart-like release in the direction of used car salesman, bankers, landlords, package tour operators, well, possibly any of those involved in fields of endeavour where the profit margin is king, kings (once), lurkers and shirkers, neighbours, priests, strangers – in Australia many of us remember the Stranger Danger Campaign, that government-backed erosion of trust in children for adults, sickening for many of us as parents, and an oblique reminder never to trust governments that appear to magnify fear. To continue: pawnbrokers, uniformed persons (some) and others in attire you would yourself not dream of wearing, even though it's worn happily by millions of others – whole populations, in fact, within patrolled borders – who, distrust being the compounding obsession it is, will match and multiply it in return and, if necessary, have plenty in reserve. Explosives to prove it.

Should we, to be thorough, and again specific, include in the list members of the medical profession? In particular, dentists? Many might have reason to think so. This being the case, I'll later consider it. But right now, at this point, distrust is far outweighing trust on the scales – according to much of the news media it's hard to see how it could be seen in any other way – and since trust, rather than its enemy is the subject of this piece and, in a civil society, the establishment of it a necessary desire, there's a need here for some hypothetical balance. No, better, a weighting in favour of trust, a sudden tilt in the scales.

For this to happen, I'll have to draw on some small-scale personal experiences, enlarge on them, recent and not so recent. Serendipitously, a short while ago, when the matter of trust had been pre-occupying me more than usual, I was witness, as an outsider, to an incident that filled me with warmth and delight. Prior to catching a flight from Budapest to London, I was standing in a queue slowly making its way towards where security would frisk and x-ray – where no-one is trusted – in the sullen silence such queues typically exhibit. When, suddenly, some members turned the queue into a party. One had a bottle of St Hubert's, a Hungarian liqueur, which in taste is what the makers of Cointreau might call a poor cousin. This bottle, amidst much hilarity, was being passed around and swigged. Now I want to make clear that I wasn't bogged down in a queue of yobs with flat-top haircuts. These were respectable-looking Hungarians, women and men, the sort a school principal, or even a policeman might defer to, their mouths open to an upended brown bottle. It was getting around fast – slow queue but quick snorts for all. That I saw this as exceptional suggested to me I'd been protected too long by living in a highly affluent, atomised country whose idea of major threat comes in the form of a few dozen desperate people in a leaky boat, heading for its coast, fleeing some tyrannical or parlous regime. In such a place germs may also be given the compliment of having a disproportionately elevated status. Threat level: high. I have witnessed middle-class Australians flee in fear from a whiff of unruly cigarette smoke. I bet well-heeled Californians do the same. Weren't these people, my fellow passengers, suspicious of becoming victims of someone else's bacteria, its ticking bomb soon to be at large in their bodies? I further recalled that where I, as a migrant, come from, arriving international passengers were once routinely sprayed with disinfectant before they could so much as get up from their seats in the plane's cabin and inhale southern hemisphere air. Here they were as careless about catching something as Phillipino child scavengers on a rubbish dump.

How sociable! How enjoyable! How trusting! I'd been in Budapest a week – on a mission involving a significant level of trust – and had come to the conclusion that Hungarians are not an exciteable people. History has robbed them of optimism. Having had, in living memory, Russian tanks and soldiers patrolling the streets will have produced that justifiably oppressive and lasting effect. Yet here they were suddenly pretty excited – preparing to leave. Who cares if some stray germ takes control of your nose! More importantly, they were trusting each other to make sure the uniformed security people didn't get their hands on, confiscate, as they'd be obliged to – mindful of terrorists – any liquid as substantial and possibly flammable as the litre bottle of St Hubert's someone, suddenly generous, had realised he'd lose. Someone blind to events, as many trusting people often are. I figured I'd trust these strangers to come to my aid in any equivalent tight jam.

In China, for instance, had they shown up when I was there. At the time I was about to put my trust into the relatively unknown – have now had several years to abbreviate the tale in conversation, set in motion prior to joining another airport queue, this one in Beijing. The Yangtze River was my goal, having abandoned my unknown-to-all-but-me protest against the massive, foolhardy, almost-completed famed dam, by not making the trip. I'd become too curious to travel the river prior to the rising of its waters – and, significantly, a several months sojourn in Beijing was swiftly coming to an end.

The arrangements were tricky – hurdling the language barriers only a part of it. There comes a point when a small repertoire of friendly greetings in Mandarin lacks muscle. You don't even need these if you are a member of a tour group, to which most tourists in the hot spots of China belong. But I've never been a good joiner – as evidenced by my lone, ineffectual and abandoned protest – am suspicious of group-think, group behaviour. Don't trust it. But trusting yourself, first and foremost, is perhaps the recourse of the damaged. If that's the case, the Chinese are not very sympathetic towards them. Independent travellers, at the beginning of the second millennium, had to be on their mettle, not because, post-Mao, there were still overt restrictions on movement, traps for the unwary, suspicions; but simply because in such a large country with its overcrowded cities, rapid change, majority poor huddling in the urban shadows of the newly wealthy, and where corruption is as endemic as transport failures, the lone Western foreigner, a weird manifestation off the beaten track to be stared at, protractedly, experiences ever-present, free-ranging unpredictability. It's as simple as that.

I'd had some prior travel experience in the Middle Kingdom. However when I was told in the concrete basement – old desk, wooden chairs, a couple of posters to convince me I was visiting a travel agent – that although I must pay for the trip along the Yangtze there and then, the ticket would later be issued to me in one of the aforementioned cities, far from Beijing, I knew that the travel experiences I'd lately had might prove to be rudimentary. I handed over a wad of renminbi notes to a woman of about my own age with memorably penetrating eyes. She, in return, gave me a receipt and an address. The effective currency of this transaction was, from my side of the desk, a lot of trust. I might have been a blasé Hungarian.

Chongqing is on the banks of the Yangtze. It has eight million inhabitants, more or less. One of them had my ticket. The airport looked ordinary enough when I arrived from Beijing, modest, no signs in English. Why should there have been? On the Air China flight we'd all watched Tom and Jerry cartoons from the sixties, dubbed in Mandarin, which I'd rather enjoyed. Strange choice, though. The little guy outsmarting the big guy: not much of that in China. Perhaps the plane was as old. It was like flying in another era. I left the terminal, hailed a taxi and showed the address, in Chinese characters, to the driver – tried to read in his face whether or not he recognised it. We sped off. I'd had some experience of green tea-sipping, intense taxi drivers and this one seemed more excitable than most. In fact, I thought he was crazy, having concluded, at the speed we were moving, that he didn't really have a clue where exactly to go. I told him, mostly by arm waving but also in the imperative mood of a language he didn't understand, to stop. He probably thought I too was crazy, so we weren't a great combination. He got the message. I got out. Another taxi approached – we'd barely left the airport – and I hailed it. What followed was a violent verbal exchange between the drivers, eye-balling each other outside their taxis, which in my understanding, as I loitered nearby – sweating, it was hot, summer approaching – concerned the fact that the first driver wanted compensation for having had his business stolen by the second driver. I didn't intervene. Eventually, they both must have realised they were wasting each others' valuable time and stormed back to their respective taxis. I was already in the new one, shoulder bag dumped in the back.

The second driver I liked much better. Behind the wheel, he was calmer. I began to trust him. More impressively, when he read the address, I felt there was a worthwhile chance that he knew its whereabouts. It seemed to cheer him up. This was obviously going to be a long ride. I settled in – worked on reducing my levels of anxiety as we sped towards the city.

Chongqing is, as I'd imagined, a very big place, sprawling over an impressive incline. To my wide and widening eyes, some of the multi-storey buildings, rather shabby, looked as if they might slide down it. Either the taxi lacked shock absorbers or, if not, they were unable to cope with the size of the ruts in the roads that lead into the labyrinthine depths of this place. I was feeling submerged. Hell-on-Earth, I thought, the dial of my emotions swinging madly to extreme. I wondered how so many people – the streets were choked with us, shuffling along, selling things, riding bikes and playing dare with the traffic – could possibly co-exist, ignore the rubbish, the stench. I was a spoilt brat in a taxi. I also wondered where in this heat I might come up for air and, more significantly, where eventually we would stop. As it happened, it was in a small side street, outside an unprepossessing concrete slab five or six storey building. I noticed, on the street, a busy rodent. More cheerfully, there was a fruit and vegetable vendor. But no indication of anything that resembled a shipping company. The taxi driver pointed to the building with conviction. I paid my fare. We shook hands.

I wasn't breathing easily yet, my full trust in the driver still incomplete. In the building there was an unlit foyer where, soon, a man in a suit appeared. From behind his glass door, he had spotted the foreigner, presumably his bewilderment as well and, oh mercy, the friendly man spoke a little English, comprehended my reason for being there. Upstairs, he said. These were outside, steel, on the back of the building, up which I bounded, knocked on a door, was admitted, saw, with hallucinatory clarity, travel posters featuring boats, a functioning office, strip lighting; took in the pretty young woman whose domain this was and then with the relief of a man surfacing from a capsized boat and grabbing a lifebuoy, pocketed with thanks the ticket she handed to me. I had been, of course, expected.

That's a deep-water analogy which had further pertinence in the nautically-themed interior. I had the ticket but there was no boat. At least, not thereabouts. A few hours later, stocked up with provisions, I was back in a taxi, this time with a woman driver who'd been instructed to locate the vessel for me, several kilometres away. I had the feeling of becoming submerged again, gripped the ticket: on it the name of the boat, my hope for surviving this unfolding travel folly which was meant to conclude with a flight from Shanghai.

Chongqing looked even grimier as dusk approached. Eventually, bones further shaken, we drove through an outlying shanty town, downhill, towards the river. In the back seat of the taxi, I was of considerable interest to the shanty town dwellers – they ran out from their grim, slapped-together structures, waving and shouting. Soon we'd have a chance to see each other at much closer range. The driver pulled up, short of the river, in the middle of about an acre of vacant bitumen. Unlike the taxi driver I'd trusted, I didn't, in view of our location, pay off this one, who'd yet to earn my trust, so fast.

The only boat I could see from our unique vantage was impressively large but seriously rusty. Drowning remained on my mind. This was an impasse. There was certainly no going forward and, now that the shipping company would be shut for the day, not much point in my going back to get fresh, correct directions. While I mulled over what to do, well, actually I was in a state of paralysis – goodness knows what options the quiet taxi driver had on her mind – the folks from the shanty town swarmed around the car, shouting what I presumed were their range of opinions about our predicament. A lot of weather-beaten, gap-toothed faces. A few skinny kids. Friendly at first, perhaps, but as the shouting got louder, I detected a developing mood of menace – wound up my window when I noticed a leathery hand on my bag. I was clearly the best diversion these people had had for a while from their appalling hardship. The river, I saw through the front windscreen, was rippling, wide and grey; a body could easily be swallowed by it at dusk. While I was reaching the climax of my intimations of drowning, a man in half a uniform – top half, semi-naval – appeared from the rusting hulk and made his way towards the commotion. The crowd, astonishingly, parted in his honour. I wound down my window. In halting English, he asked me my business. I told him. This way, he said. In half a uniform I put my trust. Shouldered my bag, paid off the driver. Followed the guy, without a backward glance towards the silenced crowd, up a tottery gangplank, crossed the decrepit deck of the hulk, leapt onto a smaller boat, previously hidden from view, crossed it to a third vessel, impressive-looking – the one named on the receipt written by the woman I'd decided to trust back in Beijing. My cabin, snug, was neatly ready. I had been, again, expected.

Other passengers, Taiwanese, somehow showed up later. They enthusiastically photographed one another against the spectacular backdrop of the Three Gorges and also, later, on our side trip in small boats to the Lesser Three Gorges, the tributary riverwaters still pristine, radiant with huge goldfish. Monkeys leapt about distantly in the surrounding lush tropical forests, thus far saved from the onslaught of human endeavour. We also saw markers showing the height to which the waters would rise, drowning riverside towns we'd visited as well as the Lesser Three Gorges. All of the photographs containing images of what now, ghostly, is under water – for the sake of Mao's trust in being able, with a grandiose plan, to conquer nature whose forces sooner or later will make their position clear – and where, for a few days, it was to my mind like surfacing into pure air during that wonderful trip.

Trust had been, step by step, sweetly rewarded. I earlier mentioned dentists – who might consider themselves to be in our debt rather than we, financially, deeply in theirs. Owe us some trust and need to return it. Some career intellectuals – if I may briefly deviate and mention another category of professional – have a field day endeavouring to make theoretically clear there's no such thing as an authentic, core self. None, it follows, to reliably trust – unless as a construct. An all-embracing theory that we're each culturally-constructed, morally creaky, post-modern assemblages is, I'd like to suggest, a clever, sedentary, desk-bound fantasy that overlooks personal experience and evidence, valued earlier by, say, William James but not by some subsequent influential thinkers whose names may not immediately come to mind when, intent on survival, your back's against the wall – which brings me again to those routine invaders of the mouth, poised to attack. Dentists are Vikings in disguise, you the patient a wretched, defenceless Anglo-Saxon – or pick your vanquisher and vanquished – mouth open, with a strong fundamental sense of the self then at stake. Not unlike an early second millennia person on his mettle, in a foreign country, when the situation is tight. It's the reason, after the drilling of a tooth, or following an extraction, we may well feel exhausted, having put a lot of primal energy into a vigorous, thwarted defence of ourselves while stretched out and suffering oral invasion. It was to a dentist I'd been, specifically, before leaving Budapest with the devil-may-care liqueur sharers.

I had a couple of reasons to be suffering from trepidation, albeit containable, when I caught the plane from London, my base, to Budapest, my dental hope. In fact more trepidation than when I was diverted by Tom and Jerry on the way to Chongqing – a trip that may have obliquely legitimised the current one. The first reason related to dentists themselves – experience had battered any original trust I had in them. As a boy in London when, compliments of the National Health Service, I first fell into the hands of dentists, they clearly saw my post-milk teeth as a source of reliable revenue. The more teeth drilled, the better to get coin from the national purse. They may even have recommended upping my daily intake of sweets. In any case, I was an early victim of that most corrosive but self-treatable condition, cynicism. It was at this time that, if I may put it this way, the rot set in.

Over the years, other dental experiences have confirmed my distrust. One dentist thought it would be a good idea if I re-mortgaged my house to facilitate his plan for my teeth. I changed dentist. Another, disbelieving the significant pain I was suffering in my lower jaw, right molar tooth, contributed significantly to my need for an enforced stay in hospital by which time I looked as if I was endeavouring to swallow a football. Emergency treatment: three days on a drip. I won't go on. It would make cheerless reading. Except to say that given my teeth have proved to be a weakness in an otherwise robust constitution, it still surprises me that I could agree to be treated by dentists with names such as Hammer and McNab (trust me, it's true) – good guys, as it turned out, but exceptions. I know dentists have the highest suicide rate among the professions, can understand this, but see no reason why they should so generously share their misery. The trip to see a dentist in Hungary forced me to draw on all of my reserves of courage, to overcome a well-established white flag mentality in the face of another odds-on defeat. The second reason for my trepidation was that, in my mind, Budapest was still behind the Iron Curtain.

So why was I putting myself through this? Because a friend in London whom I trusted recommended the clinic on the grounds that (a) he'd found the practice to be first rate and (b) dental treatment in Budapest is relatively cheap and therefore I wouldn't have to re-mortgage my house. I should add a (c): necessity and even a (d): I hadn't visited an eastern European country before. All up, it was compelling. I had a work-free week, a passport, a *Lonely*

*Planet Guide* – and the absurd possibility of having trust, resurgent, further nursed back into me, thanks to my teeth.

When you embark on do-it-yourself repairs or renovations – in the mortgaged house – or trust a builder or carpenter to wreak havoc on the normal household routine, dust everywhere, electricity cut, in the hope of a sound outcome, it's necessary to work around the temporary catastrophe. It's the same getting teeth re-upholstered. When not at my hotel, happily reading, or at the clinic, grimly submitting, I wore out a lot of leather getting my bearings in Budapest: visited art and history museums, discovered antiquarian bookshops, caught trams as much to gather the mood and demographic – strange, having come from London, to be among whites only – as to arrive at a destination. Saw the wide, impressive Danube, dividing Buda from Pest, from many vantages. Ate, or rather, drank goulash, such a delicious soup (I was going for soft food) and not the kind of stew proposed in my childhood by the likes of Mrs Beeton and others in far-off regions untroubled by the down home specifics in land-locked Hungary. As predicted by what I'd read, I saw the pock marks from Soviet bullets in the facades of old buildings – and people with determined-looking faces who might have heard the bullets. But what had especially caught my interest, in preparation for the trip, were the thermal pools.

I should now write to the folks at Lonely Planet: their guide to Budapest, third edition, is not to be completely trusted. It's good on the geology of the area – the fact that it's on a fault line and, as a consequence of the abundant underground water, boasts hot thermal springs. Good too on how they've been harnessed for human advantage. There are indoor thermal bathing pools at various points in the compass throughout the city. The one I was going to visit soon after I arrived and then planned to re-visit on subsequent days is one of the oldest, erected in 1570, when Hungary was part of the Ottoman Empire. I was curious about the building – a survivor in a city that has suffered much turmoil and wreckage – and had noted that it was conveniently close to my hotel.

I'd mentioned its name, Király, to the dentist. He is a man who speaks several languages and had told me, during an initial consultation in London, that aristocrats in ancient Egypt who had lost a tooth would hi-jack one from a servant as a replacement, in the form of a dental bridge. I'd never before met a dentist who exhibited such an historical depth of knowledge about his profession. It impressed me – fed my confidence in him. He was interested, too, in my activities around Budapest. The visit to the baths followed two hours in his surgery, supine, under the bright, facilitating lights.

The baths were dim and shabby. After parting with some florint notes, I was told I'd have to wear what looked like an apron made of white cloth – not the bathers I'd brought – and to change in one of the cubicles. It was a men only day, men and women only days being what was strictly on offer. I changed out of my clothes then locked the door of the cubicle behind me and made for the baths, down some stairs. Light was not at a premium anywhere in this building. The main pool was under what the *Lonely Planet Guide* describes as 'a wonderful skylit dome'. Certainly its age made it impressive and, back when the Turks assembled it, the meagre amount of light admitted through its small, circular openings might have been impressive too. Nowadays it is assisted by a few wall lights, thwarted by opaque orange glass. I descended, an obvious novice, down stone steps into the pool.

It was only wide enough for about four or five swimming strokes. Anyway, none of the men, widely varying in age, were swimming. The form was to sit on the wide underwater stone terraces, maybe talk, and let the warm steamy water take its effect. Fresh water gushed from a pipe. The stone walls were as wet as the bathers when leaving the pool. There were also small, rectangular shaped baths set next to the walls but I kept to the pool, intent on relaxation though bothered intermittently by the unpredictability of the apron.

There were also a couple of saunas. I noticed that for most of the punters, the idea was to alternate between the pool and the sauna. Visibility in the one I chose was low. The heat, predictably, was impressive. The seating arrangements involved three tiers of wooden seats to sit on and sweat profusely. On the lowest one, there was a space where, after an awkward adjustment of my apron, I sat. The wood was exceedingly hot. The steam was thick but not thick enough, when I made a necessary choice to stand, to hide what I initially disbelieved but later confirmed. When I returned to the pool the water seemed cool. On the wall was a clock. I'd been there for an engrossing but slow forty minutes.

One further visit to the sauna, I thought, working on my confidence. It was standing room only; the seats were now fully occupied. Not only crowded but also, I became dimly then clearly aware, now physically very active. I'd entered this establishment to chill out – to briefly join an assumed tradition dating back several centuries. It seemed the right time and place. As it happened, this was the right time and place but, clearly, the tradition was to indulge in the erotic benefits available when attending men only sessions. A successful and thriving tradition – perhaps also extending to women's days, there being equal opportunity. Though for me, in mid-repair – and in any case, as stated earlier, a reluctant group participant – a combined men's and women's day, similarly frisky, in this now insufficiently dimly lit public place would not have attracted me. You don't have to pay or wear a silly white apron to enter a bedroom. I was glad to be shot of the garment, tossed it into the designated bin when, after quitting the sauna, a little shaken, I changed, and left the ancient building which, remarkably, no victor, German or Russian, had flattened, unlike its neighbours, all recent.

I checked my *Lonely Planet Guide* to Hungary. It's gay and lesbian section requires revision before I'm tempted to trust, unswervingly, the book's other observations and advice. My dentist on the day of my departure, now that I was complete with teeth that could tackle the toughest cut of Hungarian beef, was surprised by the guide's oversight. The pool and its reputation are well known

– in Budapest. My well-travelled dentist, not only an expert in his field but also with broad and tolerant views, said he could have enlightened me about Király but, not being privy to my lack of knowledge or sexual proclivities, felt he was at risk of causing possible offence. All I could think, while confidently departing from his well-staffed, cheerful and shining clinic, was that this caution on my behalf was very decent and considerate.

In a restaurant, after a good meal, I'm of those who'll send compliments to the chef; to a dentist, in whom I've placed trust that's been rewarded, a testimonial. These surely add to the overall, potential bank of trust for sharing around, not always guaranteed but surely a bank worth investing in, given that trust can be so easily squandered by us all. And it's a fact: trust attracts financial metaphors – self-interest thereby made prominent – and certainly more often than in relation to other personal qualities we may value. You've got to put your trust in something, we hear people say, implying it is nowhere evident what the something to trust in might be or that it is merely a fickle phantom to be grabbed at in passing. I don't trust these people. They must be wilfully blind as to where exactly to gain or provide it.

# ON BEING TRANSPORTED

A third of the world's shoes are now made annually in a megalopolis in southern China, Guangzhou – millions, perhaps billions of shoes. It's a warm up for exhaustion to imagine all of the walking to myriad destinations – most often shops – those shoes will improve, north, south, east and west on the planet, and how quickly, once the thin soles are worn through or the uppers split, countless more shoes will speed from the production lines, ready for export. Then to consider how a mere few millennia ago we as a species, roaming in predatory groups, had yet to succumb to the comforts of even a single pair of animal-skin footwear. As I write this, bare feet under the table, my own favoured shoes or, more specifically, boots are at the repairer.

I don't rely on container ships from China to supply me with footwear but (I assume) road haulage from nearby South Australia where there's a comparatively small factory that makes Rossi boots, family run since 1910. They have been my footwear of choice for the past fifteen years. Reasons: quality, comfort, plain style – and, especially, because the tough soles are stitched not moulded to the leather upper. This means that when the soles are worn through they can be replaced; I don't have to jettison the boots, wastefully, each time the few thousand kilometres the soles are good for have been crossed.

Rossi boots are relatively expensive; the rewarding compensation is longevity and, after a purchase, instant affection. Furthermore, not being the owner of a car – at least not for fifteen years – the acquisition of a pair of high quality boots seems a thoroughly justifiable favour to bestow on myself since, inside cities, I'm likely to cover more territory on foot than most. I like walking for its own sake – for the physical wellbeing and mental clarity that come with it.

I'm currently missing my pair of Rossi boots. No wonder, now I'm at the brief mercy of some inferior substitutes, my thoughts have turned to transport, George Stephenson, the Wright Brothers, Henry Ford – those guys you heard about at school while itching with simian restlessness to get outside and move about – and other inventors and manufacturers in the business of relieving us of the pleasures of perambulation, rare beside the busy highways that connect modern cities. Transport shapes their geographies (I bet Guangzhou is no exception) and the way we view and experience them. A city-dweller for most of my life, I have spent approximately a third of it in each of three cities, big and small – with the possibility of additional comparison arising from having strayed into others, in various countries, boots or shoes ever airing under a temporary bed.

1

I am writing this in Melbourne, well-known home, in Australia, of the tram – can hear them trundling past on the street, a main artery. It's a comforting sound, especially at night, of ritual transience. But right now, I'm recalling the capital city of the island to the south where, by the time I first went there, and stayed, trams were for the locals a memory – passenger trains as well. Hobart, Tasmania, is where I bought my first pair of Rossi boots. A city, population 210,000, situated between a deepwater estuary and a mountain perceived by some inhabitants as exhibiting grandeur, by others an imposing dark presence – perhaps once seen as threatening, like a brute overseer, to a convict in chains – therefore a matter of personal temperament, the mountain unmoved. You might think sales of footwear would be a thriving retail business for a population of walkers entranced by a version of the memorable location. It's not evident. Until a few years ago the city did boast a long-established boot manufacturer, Blundstone, rival to Rossi, now gone, possibly to China. However, car dealers, new and used, thrive – as do gloomy multi-storey car parks, evidence of the lure of a day out in town and the general desire to experience a place of variable and sometimes wild weather from a cocoon: you don't feel geographically remote, north of Antarctica, in a line of cars.

Trams were expelled from the streets – narrower than Melbourne's, the result of an earlier less visionary colonial plan – many decades ago. The vehicles were finally done for after one of them sped headlong down the incline of the north/south main street, the driver clanging his bell normally used to indicate imminent departure but now suddenly a failure of breaks, the many lives he saved at the expense of his own, a hero's.

This is not a town renowned for the safety of getting to and from and about it. Ask any cyclist (I'm an ex-cyclist there) who's been shaken by the gale of a log-truck barrelling down Davey Street, past the waterfront, or who has clipped if not run into, since it's so easy, one of the many car doors so carelessly opened – sudden obstacles to arrival, a modest and otherwise safe distance away, without injury. Such humiliation, or worse, a local consequence it seems of private motorists' slavish views that the internal combustion engine now has an exclusive right at street-level – forget the unpunctual buses – to power restless civilisation's best loved invention. This is what happens when other means of wheeled transport become history. To cap it off, such dangers arise after, with a certain amount of heavy breathing or freewheeling, the hapless Hobart cyclist will likely have experienced some of the steepest gradients of any city on earth known to boast of its must-see location. For that attribute it's up there with other island harbour cities such as Valletta in Malta or St John's in Newfoundland, best experienced in the enduring comfort and reliability of a pair of good leather boots, Rossi's or others.

I confess, however, that I too as a driver have been the cause of potential danger, easy in Hobart. It has an interesting and, to the newcomer, abstruse mixture of one-way and two-way streets. They might have been so organised to fool and upset interlopers – and do. Just ask a tourist in a hire-car what on his first day in town gave his experience of it an edge.

Back when I first arrived, I drove a temperamental white Volkswagen which, because of its mechanical moods, sometimes distracted my attention from the roads on which I was driving. I thought, and so did my future wife, that my transgression on a relatively quiet day – who'd know in the circumstances which way the traffic was meant to be flowing? – having aroused no more than a small swarm of oncoming horns (none of them from a police car) before I braked hard and executed a quick manoeuvre into a camouflage of parked cars, would soon be no more remarked upon than the bitumen. Weeks later, at a party, the matter of personal transport somehow arising, a guest to whom we confessed we had an old bomb was then delighted to let us know that it must have been us newcomers she'd recently seen break the law. Amazed to be so visible, so visibly dangerous, the place so interconnected, the impulse might have been to fill the tank, make an escape to the ferry and board it back to the mainland. Oddly, it wasn't. Instead, we chose to hunker down and face the many trials, vehicular and social.

The foregoing is not the only distinctive feature of traffic flow in Hobart. The urban population is divided by the River Derwent as it broadens into an estuary; a hump-shaped bridge connects the two shores. It too presents danger, being in all probability the only non-swing bridge in the world to be closed to traffic when doing what it is supposed to do, allow a ship of substance to pass under it. That is, until recently – when pilot boats began to guide looming vessels. Stuck in a queue, perhaps in a fume on the way to the airport, drivers have been reminded of the time in 1975 – if then they were alive – when an ore carrier, the Lake Illawarra, collided with the bridge one foggy evening. The ship sank, part of the bridge collapsed, and cars fatally unaware of the event (there were none on the missing stretch of the span at the time) plunged into the dark water below. Others, photos attest, teetered on the edge of the void and remained there until daylight, long after their terrified passengers had fled. Each precautionary closure of the bridge to traffic has provided compulsory time for those in the queues of cars to reflect upon this tragedy; a safe crossing – a hollow feeling recurrent on the repaired section – frequently provides a sense of relief. At least, that's my experience.

If you have flown to Hobart by plane, your drive or bus-ride from the airport will reach its conclusion with a crossing of the vulnerable Tasman Bridge, and from it there's a fine view of the large botanical gardens. Beyond them, on the other side of the rise, some of it bushland (known curiously as the Queen's Domain) is a group of houses known collectively as the Glebe, once church property. Its streets heading down towards the city are predictably steep. This didn't put me off buying a small nineteenth-century terrace house at the top of one of them. Ascending cars sometimes struggle to gain traction in the wet and their tyres shriek – cyclists, unless they are Olympians, simply alight from their bikes.

Before the common advent of either of those forms of transport, a friend of mine's great-grandfather owned a company that hired horse-drawn coaches in the area. Back then, the survivors of the wrecked native tribes who once roamed the island in their own sensible time still existed within living memory. One afternoon, my friend told me, a small group of inebriated spectators from the Tasmanian Cricket Ground – located not far from the top of my street – hired a coach and four, his forebear in the box seat, hands on the reins. These he'd lost a grip on by the time the coach sped downwards, past my house – lazing in the sun on my front verandah, I used to visualise it – having himself had a tipple too many. This might have been newsworthy, broken limbs or worse – I imagine that from the coach each house in my street appeared to quake violently given the no doubt well-touted smooth reliability of the hired conveyance, and the collaborating influence of drink. Had the departing spectators made a wise choice and left on foot, no such unnecessary illusion would have shocked them. As it happened, before the coach and four hurtled towards certain calamity at the T-junction below, the forebear had the presence of mind and a special relationship with one of the horses to call it, thus influencing the rest, to an eventual, dust-raising halt. Even now the incident remains testimony to the implications of making haste in the region – still talked of in remarkably fast, gossip-oiled Hobart.

2

Beneath the agitations of traffic, in trains underground, you get to be intimate with fellow citizenry, especially in London and particularly during rush-hour. Tube trains are not for the claustrophobic or frail. Jammed in, standing, you know if the woman pushed next to you has recently brushed her teeth or the bloke with his nose close to your ear has just left the pub. The spirit of co-operation – evidence that along with ants and bees we can be one of the most co-operative species on earth, under some conditions – is admirable though, of course, everyone complains. Then, next day, everyone's back, burrowing under the city on a line that is part of the first underground train network in the world. New Yorkers or Berliners may scoff at the conditions – faintworthy in summer – but it was a highly evolved system from the beginning: it still works. Indeed, those down on their luck, wondering where the next bed might be found, especially in winter, find the seating, temperature, overall conditions second-to-none, board at a chosen station on the Circle Line and revolve under London all day.

When the network was built, one of the great engineering feats of the Victorian age, no-one could have envisioned the exponential growth of the city and the future stress on metropolitan sensibility, as millions of workers and tourists flock under ground. Exhausted, trains and signals seize up and so, occasionally, do citizens, suddenly in need of escorting. It's an indication of the pressure London's overall transport infrastructure is potentially under, and the fragility of the co-operation so evident on the Underground – though you'd have to shout the news to the many consumers attuned to their Ipods – that, at any one time, the city is only nine meals away from anarchy. Or so I've read. In the light of this ever-possible though fortunately as yet untested threat, finding a seat and opening a book to read in a tube train, among other passengers reading or listening or dozing, slack-jawed, quieter now that it's evening, seems an experience not to be taken for granted, or the time squandered in finding fault with the air conditioning.

It's rare to have a conversation, or make eye-contact with a stranger on the tube unless, with the train inexplicably stalled in the tunnel, there are urgent whispers about a bomb scare. We're in the Old World where social barriers remain stubbornly and, amazingly to some, still largely in place. Here's a conversation I had a little while back with a fortyish black guy sitting next to me who'd, with a nudge, interrupted my reading. My legs were crossed.

Him: Are you gay?
Me: I beg your pardon?
Him: I said, are you gay?
Me: It's none of your business.
Him: Come on, man, are you?
Me: This is ridiculous.
Him: Are you?
Me: If I was, I'd see no reason to tell you.
Him: I bet you are.
Me: You can bet what you like.
Him: Are you?
Me: I don't see that it matters one way or the other.
Him: (Silent, looking at me, broad smile).
Me: No, as it happens.
Him: Well, that's cool too.
Me: Great! So pleased to hear it! Cheerio.

I'd arrived at my station – surprised on hurriedly alighting to have enjoyed this extempore meeting with the absurdly intrusive and cheerful stranger, others keenly listening in. It was refreshing. But that's life under ground: unpredictable when there's a sudden crack in the ever battered codes of established behaviour.

Above ground there'd be more chance – if one wished to – of immediately fleeing from such an encounter. What's more fares on overground public transport can be much cheaper. For a quid you can ride on a bus from one side of London to the other, no disembarkation at such a steal permitted. If I were a tourist, I'd think this a magnificent investment – a way of both seeing the famous sights that good fortune had blessed the particular route with and experiencing the unpredictable quotidian. Potentially tough competition for London cabbies, each of whom could find the obscure laneway, wide enough for a seventeenth-century hand-pulled cart, off Fleet Street where Samuel Johnson lived, as effortlessly as a gravitationally impelled drop of mercury, slipping past hazards, will settle upon a destination like a full stop. Therefore, as it happens, no contest. Ask a celebrity, a wad of tenners handy, fleeing from the paparazzi. If time is a significant consideration, better to go with the driver who has The Knowledge, and tip him, than risk getting stuck on a bus in the Old Kent Road without adequate supplies of food and drink – a fine if you're tempted to be sustained by them and get caught – and some personal entertainment, once a book or a newspaper, now one of their technological enemies.

Among those citizens who are forbearing enough to make use of buses – the cash-strapped majority – there are some for whom two seats, either side of the aisle, are particularly coveted. I am thinking here of the double-decker bus not its inferior, single tier, red-Ducoed relative that in the society of London buses a person might condescend to fraternise with and catch, though, from a preferred vantage, it would be looked down upon. The seats are those up at the front, top deck. Ever since I was a boy, born to be a Londoner, bounding up the stairs, I've felt keen disappointment if other passengers have got to them first. From those seats I had my first tentative experience – thrill – of travelling a long few miles from home, alone. Afternoons would find them mostly unoccupied, our outer London district a place to survey from a wonderful height. The pleasure of sitting up there, poised to observe, to feel the moving bus sway, has never left me.

From the seats, over the decades, during periods when I've lived in London again, I've seen the city change, though frequently, now there are so many more cars, more impatience, rage, it's as quick or quicker to hoof it, take a route better suited to a pair of durable

Rossi boots. Or lash out and catch the tube, perhaps to surface, a brisk last-minute sprint up an escalator, in one of the grand Victorian stations, St Pancras, Paddington, Euston, names synonymous with the steam that obscured those monuments to the days of Empire – and all of the separations, reunions, escapes.

## 3

After we arrived in Melbourne from London as migrants, the trains that caught our family attention, and occasionally attracted our fares, were known affectionately as 'red rattlers' which, a decade later, in the seventies, would begin to be replaced. These electric trains were wooden bodied with saloon compartments, pressed metal ceilings, luggage racks at head-height above the opposing seats. They were dangerous. If you were so disposed, and a schoolboy, you could hang out of the sash windows while the train was in motion – I dimly recall stories, possibly apocryphal and judged to put the wind up a migrant, of gruesome fatalities – but better than this, you could thrillingly hop off the running board before the train had come to a halt. I expect there was a sign saying something like 'Do not alight while the train is in motion', an invitation to be disobedient.

Disobedience was rife. I think the carriage doors were made to slide, so it's odd that I seem to recall the sound of them slamming, an imported memory attached to the rattlers – or as likely I'm hearing the terminal slamming of doors on compartments of my memory. Whether sliding or swing, these doors existed in the days before a form of blanket Western authoritarianism relieved the individual of having the choice of either jumping off the train while it was still in motion or carefully alighting from it at a station by dictating that escape from travel confinement must be through doors of the automatic variety. The days of grazed knees, the dare, and chase consequent upon being late for a departure were largely over.

Not quite, not, at least in the wide streets of Melbourne. While the citizens of Amsterdam may have been seasonably glad to be automatically sealed inside their smart new trams while the canals were frozen, Melbourne's breezy trams – sliding doors often casually left open – remained the bane of newspaper readers. Readers, in Melbourne, are legion, as any tram ride may well reveal; the trams now mostly of the sealed-doors-for-your-safety variety, though a few renegades remain in service for old time's sake. Obedience – mostly – flourishes, remarkable in a city composed significantly of folk or their immediate forebears who migrated from countries where attitudes to the rules of the road are often random. I know, as I sit here barefoot – my Rossi boots by now in an advanced state of repair – within earshot of trams trundling along tracks down the middle of the road, that when each of them stops for passengers, the traffic going in the same direction will stop in sympathy, until all of the passengers are safely on board or safe on the pavement and the tram moves on. I know equivalent rituals in Rome would be more excitably negotiated and, to counter any perceived bias in singling out that spirited city, not Rome alone.

In case I have given the impression that the citizens of Melbourne have become a spineless, compliant lot – though it's sometimes true of the armies of Lycra-wearing, headlong cyclists abusing T-shirted riders who reject the necessity of wearing regulation helmets – I should point out that on trams fare evasion is known to be common. Call an unpaid fare ride theft, if you must, but more charitably it's a protest against the replacement of conductors by ticket machines not equipped to spot a true recidivist, help protect a peaceable passenger from a truculent drunk, or offer a steadying hand down the steps to the less able in a rapidly ageing population. All matters of little or no interest to the ubiquitous reader, heading for work or home, deep in sophisticated concentration.

I was on a tram going home a year or so ago, mid-evening, wine on my breath after an exhibition opening, when from my standing position – the tram was unusually crowded for the time of day – I noticed a man, seated, reading what appeared to be a collection of poems, judging from the arrangement of words on the pages.

Guesswork, I was standing at a distance. It's rare enough these days to spot anyone reading poetry, even in a library, except possibly on a tram in the city of Melbourne. I edged closer to see if I could identify the book the guy was reading.

At the time, I'd developed a sudden and passionate enthusiasm for the songs of the American singer-songwriter, Warren Zevon – a belated result of having read a long elegy by Paul Muldoon, both for Zevon and Muldoon's sister. I'd read it in the *TLS* but eventually it appeared in a poetry collection, *Horse Latitudes*. I'd wondered why on earth Muldoon had expended so much energy and invention on a dead singer whom I'd disparagingly considered to be an obscure one-hit wonder. The song: 'Werewolves of London'. The poem, arresting because of its verbal pyrotechnics, didn't make it remotely clear to me; Muldoon seemed to be more interested in his poem than in Zevon. Eventually, I chanced upon a copy of Zevon's last album, made while he was dying of cancer, listened to it and thereafter bought all of the rest, entranced by his noirish wit and compositional brilliance, voice and musicianship – one of the albums containing fine lyrics by Muldoon.

You don't need to have heard of the undervalued Zevon or the rarefied Muldoon – in all likelihood there were only two passengers on this particular tram and quite possibly on any tram then running who had heard of them both, though I hope not – to by now have gathered that a galvanic, co-incidental encounter was in the offing. I now saw that the seated guy, as he closed the book thus revealing the cover, the woman sitting next to him suddenly rising to leave the tram, happened to be reading *Horse Latitudes*. I quickly sat next to him.

I'm not prone to be like the cheerfully intrusive black guy on the London underground train except, surely, when I've had a glass or two of wine – and besides things are looser here, less socially constricted.

'Not often you come across someone reading poems on a tram,' I said, eyeing the bag in which he had placed the book. 'Paul

Muldoon, especially,' I added trying to sound a bit knowledgeable, not mad.

'No,' he said, suspicious but polite, 'I guess not.'

'*Horse Latitudes*.'

'Yes. You read it?'

'I have – a while back.'

'Well, that's amazing.'

'Eh?'

'That you know the book.' Responsive, accommodating white guy amazed that either I had prior knowledge of the slim volume or a super-sensory vision of the book now hidden in his bag.

'Not really,' I said, quietly. This was Melbourne. I don't think he heard me.

'Just read the last poem…'

'The one about Warren Zevon and…'

'Yeah, 'Sillyhow Stride'.'

'Do you know who Warren Zevon is?' I asked.

'Warren Zevon…' long pause, indicative of significance '…Warren Zevon is God.'

Now that shook me.

His estimation I didn't have time and the presence of mind to concur with or challenge before, suddenly realising and indicating that the tram had come to a halt at his stop, the guy grabbed his bag, stood up, moved to alight and then disappeared into the warm night. Short of my destination, I remained seated a while longer in replete, meditative silence staring in wonder, it might have been specifically, down at my boots – the marvellous Rossis I'm now set to collect from the repairer, eight stops on the afternoon tram, then a well-shod, brisk walk or dawdle back home.

# ON SELF-KNOWLEDGE

On the little finger of my left hand is a ring that fits snugly. It's been there for a decade. I began to wear it several years after my father died. Then, a few days ago, I was washing my oily hands in hot water – I'd been cooking a fish dish – and the ring slipped off. This had never happened before. I'm staying in lodgings in London – though they go by some flashier name – and the basin I was using lacked a plug, the metal sort you manipulate up and down via a lever behind the central hot and cold tap. The ring shot straight down the plughole. It is a gold band joined in a buckle, known as a keeper ring. I didn't think this would happen either: I am the third member of my family to wear it, first my grandfather, then my father, now me. Or should I say, then me. The last. The ring had gone. I looked down the plughole and saw only darkness; imagined the heirloom plummeting down the narrow pipe – I'm on the third floor – into some tributary, water rushing through it towards a main artery in the vast subterranean network of London's sewers. The only hope of its rescue – but not by me – being that it might stall in one of the old Victorian pipes undergoing seemingly endless replacement, and be prized by its sweating finder, though most likely he'd have thicker fingers than mine. Otherwise, it was as good as vaporised.

What struck me was that I accepted the loss. I'd inherited the ring, worn it for a while, now it was gone. History. What happens. At most, I felt a bit forlorn. This is not what I would have imagined feeling had the incident been hypothetical. I'd surely have conceived then that my mind would start racing, as fast as the ring, towards upset, distress. A flood of feeling. Who was this person, six decades alive endeavouring to be commonly wise, a representative believer in self-examination, for myself and for the sake of others – indeed, a believer in knowing myself, lizard brain included, its existence the reason why we are so riveted by wild, fellow creatures, birds or reptiles, whether threatened by or attracted to them – who was this cool, civilised stranger staring dumbly down a dark plughole where something significant had dropped?

I assume my father began to wear the ring, also on his left little finger, in 1953, the year his father died. I think he admired him. The men in my family have the hands of clerks not labourers, slender fingers to pass on the gold band. But I always thought, with its buckle, it looked masculine, not an adornment – exhibiting strength not foppery. What it first represented for my grandfather – assuming he was the first wearer – I don't know. He was a major in the British army on the administrative side, an accountant, not the only buckle he would wear. The one on his finger was part of a man's solid ring, of its time. Over the years countless molecules of gold have been rubbed off, and even when I was a boy the delineations of the buckle were smoothed. Soft gold. I wanted to hold it. On my father's finger it represented continuity, even authority, when there was family turbulence.

Now I had lost it, not far from where I spent my childhood. When very young I could not have conceived that I'd never want to wear it; that after my father had died in 1996, I'd reject its weight on my finger, having tried the ring on, as a thing I'd have to shake off. The weight of decades, for the widower and his son, of mutual impatience and blame, erosion of respect, words not said, kindnesses not built upon – mutually tough dependence like the tongue of a belt in its buckle. Or, perhaps, mutual need of each other, blood-tied in a psychological grapple, no time limit, age eventually on my side. How could such a survivor suddenly wear the very thing that would signal a victory?

Eventually, I did wear it. It happened this way, unexpectedly. Do we best discover knowledge of ourselves when caught unawares? I'd returned the keeper ring to the small, blue pull-top bag supplied by the funeral director, stored it in a drawer, and mostly forgot about it. Later, because I was going away for a long time, the ring and countless other items were stored in the roof of my house, prior to it being leased. When I returned, five or six years after the funeral, down came the stuff again – and I spotted the little cloth bag. I opened it, inspected the ring, tried it on, idly, little finger, left hand. It felt right. I left it there. Why? What had happened? I slowly realised that I'd changed but hadn't kept up with the pace. The change was subterranean, faster flowing than I could have conceived. Proof the self can be ever transforming – shadows capable of changing to shine. It struck me: I had become reconciled to my father without really knowing it. Now it was my little finger that burnished the inside of the ring.

Those years when the ring had been stored in the cloth bag, a forgotten thing, I'd been leading a partly secret life: conversing with myself about my father, indeed, sometimes, internally talking to him. Long ago I'd realised that I was never going to treat my own children in the way my father had treated me. Cut out the fear, nurture the seeds of encouragement. Let affection bloom. Now I'd begun to see him, from a distance in time, in his own right free of what I'd encouraged in him – so different to what my daughters have encouraged in me, and who loved him, that isolated, stoical man who never complained about his lot. Who would drown overcooked meat and two veg in a lake of gravy and be convinced that no finer meal could be ordered in any restaurant; who on a par three sank two holes-in-one in a single week but spent much of his time in the rough; who considered the hand-sized huntsman spiders he shared his house with to be his 'friends'; who smoked a pipe; who lived, after I left home, ever alone; who being a fit, determined, punctual man, never took a day off work during his forty-four years as an actuary, except for my mother's funeral in 1962; who had been a prodigy in mathematics; who, a lone campaigner for correctness, made lists of words whose pronunciations Australians, in his view, mangled; who wrote published letters to Melbourne's *Age*; whose eyebrows were long and wild; who once drew a wounded bull on a Cabcharge receipt and said, to my daughters, that's how they charge; who was a whiz at cryptic crosswords; who loved whisky; who lived and wore, on his left little finger, a gold keeper ring.

It was gone. I thought the upset must surely come later. The loss. I looked down the plughole again, then realised that in my pocket was a keyring torch. I was glad nobody chanced to spot me so carefully examining the facilities which, if the owners are honest with themselves, require some capital outlay. To my astonishment, I spotted the glinting rim of the ring – saved from a freefall by an obstruction, a nail or something. I was no longer fatalistic or forlorn but seized by the need for rapid action, ran to get that most protean artefact, a coathanger, unwound the neck, stretched the length of the wire straight, made a crude hook at one end and, nervously, lowered it. I'd been fooling myself when I accepted the loss: shocked. Now I was attempting surgical precision, a make or break manoeuvre, wire in one hand, tiny torch in the other. The ring shifted promisingly then slipped past the obstruction. But not, amazingly, out of sight. It hadn't occurred to me that the downpipe would be U-shaped – what ignorance we can live with! Now, should any witness have been about, I was a novice plumber, crouching, engaged in frantic dismantling, heavy breathing. The ring! Soon I had it in my hand and a lot of water on the tiled floor – had what the ring represents, and a reassertion of the importance of it. In the future I hope one of my grandsons will choose to wear the gold keeper and, hey, even flash it.

# ON CURIOSITY

For the curious, curiosity about one thing leads to curiosity about another – a link is made and soon there's a chain of connections. Hand to a susceptible child a fossil, a ubiquitous trilobite, for instance, follow it up with an introduction to geology and this might be the beginning for him or her of a lifetime interest in clambering about fossil cliffs, noticing rock strata and rock composition, and visiting Natural History Museums. You, curious, will notice such a person hanging around the edge of an excavation site for the foundations of a new big building – or getting as close as she can to where the drilling through the rock of the region is going on – and wonder what can be so preoccupying about an inner city crater apart from the unbearable racket.

There is a difference, of course, between curiosity, fresh and lively, and its dubious relative, obsessive interest, which encourages those it inhabits to pace up and down. The obsessed are not prone to ask questions – perhaps because they are fully exercised by the knowledge that no-one other than themselves is fit to nail the necessary answers. Such a person will be of significant interest, even concern, to a person who is curious. It is she who will ask questions about everything from the composition of a leaf to the social and architectural genius of ants, aware such matters will remain something of a mystery no matter what she discovers as, indeed, most things always will. Forget the conversation killer beneath the stars: why is there something rather than nothing? Black holes will be enough to be getting on with for the evening.

Curiosity, we know, developed as a natural consequence of our emerging human consciousness – but what, in its own unique way, a rock for instance, isn't somehow consciously responsive to its surroundings? – evolving languages, evolving with languages, now at our service. For those of us who don't have the superstructure of an organised religion within which to inhabit the mystery of being – compass and updated maps provided by the priestly classes – the revolving Earth's orbit around our favourite hurtling star is a wobbling mystery ride, humans no more privileged than any other sentient beings on board, or trees. Except that we ask questions and for us, theoretical physicists currently in the front line, the answers inevitably spark fresh questions. Without end? If they create decent sparks. I gather geologists have yet to comprehend how flint, that maker of actual sparks, forms in limestone regions. Flint and the origin of the universe both have something in common, a definite connection, especially for the curious.

Most of us satisfy our curiosity not by endeavouring to solve significant mysteries – unless we've been cuckolded or robbed – or even, in these days of twenty-four hour passive and pacifying mass entertainment, by reading books. It's mostly by seeking experiences: eyes, nose, tongue, ears, fingertips greedy for immediacies. I remember how at one time most of the world seemed hopelessly out of reach; the sea, only a summer holiday away, marvellously within it. But there was a lot of sea between where I was in London and what as a young boy I'd spotted in photographs, most likely in a geography text book, my favourite subject at school. From that day, and I'm sure there was a particular day, geysers and monkeys were always associated – connected – in my mind. I don't know if I thought visiting the geysers in Rotorua, New Zealand would lead inevitably to the sighting of a troop of monkeys but I do know I thought it very unlikely I'd ever see either. But since that day, the desire to see both never left me – those black and white photos never faded. I wanted to see their subjects in action.

There could be no hurry. While I didn't know my parents and I were soon to fly much closer to both, the monkeys and geysers remained connected by remoteness. Even so, it would take two decades for the improbable – always good at helping to sustain curiosity – suddenly to happen, fortuitously and not by design, no doubt because during the intervening years countless other matters of curiosity had taken priority; curiosity magnified in the company of fellow humans whose remote forebears migrated from Africa out of dietary necessity, certainly, though I imagine that's not the only reason their heavy brows were furrowed above eyes fixed on the unfamiliar terrain that lay ahead.

I encountered the geysers first. It was after attending a conference I'd been invited to in Palmerston North – tantalisingly close to Rotorua. The pungent smell of sulphur, a blast, banished what I remembered of the photo. Here was primordial nature, visibly active, potentially violent – the planet refusing to act the mature age it does elsewhere. Seeing steaming geysers shoot up, tree height, with virile frequency, was tremendously exciting – though I was told the length and height of these ejaculations were even greater before thermally produced electricity sapped their force. There was drifting steam in all directions – and paths to follow strictly, sulphur accumulating around hissing fumeroles. Deep pools, blue – the day was sunny – looked enticing until, at their edge, it was clear they were boiling, smooth water always about to swell or bubble. A man who fell into one of them – true? – was never seen again. But what he left behind was the thrill of ever-to-be-courted danger. Mud in pools behaved as mud doesn't, usually, like a very thick taupe soup, subterranean heat exciting it. Globs of the mud leapt up and flopped. It swallowed itself. Listening to this was to be in the neighbourhood of a flatulence problem. This mud was promoted as being good for the skin. Before I forced myself to leave all of this lively expression of energy – I felt re-energised myself – I bought from a shop two dry mudpacks for the woman I loved on the other side of the Tasman Sea.

She was with me, however, in Ubud, Bali when I encountered the monkeys. In fact, you'll be curious to discover, she became a star there. But that was after the encounter – which happened in what is known as the Monkey Forest, an enjoyable walk away from where we were staying. That walk was a must. When on that hot and steamy day we arrived at the forest there was no sign of the creatures we had come to see. But eventually there was movement in the higher branches of the trees, gymnastics among the vines.

We were standing in a clearing, watching a troop of long-tailed macaques. I wanted to get much closer but at the same time didn't want to frighten them off. In any case, we'd been cautioned: they carry disease, they bite. No wonder, the Balinese throw stones at them, part of a complex and not always hostile relationship.

Closer to where they were, there was a large log – perhaps dragged into the clearing – and, luckily, few other tourists. We'd arrived as a couple; now it was my turn to do something on my own. I figured if I quietly sat on the log for a while, the macaques might pay their respects. Already, by now, some were loping about on the ground. It didn't take long. In my anticipation, I almost forgot about the heat, my soaking T-shirt. I was joined by half-a-dozen macaques of varying ages and sizes.

These are not large monkeys, so when you have one on your shoulder there is no problem. One on each shoulder is fine too. Having half-a-dozen clambering over you – one, admittedly, still in the nursery – is more interesting. Sitting there, letting them inspect me, I knew I mustn't alarm them by any sudden movement, perhaps any movement at all. I didn't want to be bitten. I didn't want them to go. They have beautiful round, alert brown eyes. We looked at each other; they seemed as curious about me as I was of them. We had more than genetic composition in common: fleas. One of the monkeys thought I might have some, so began to search through my hair, not a big task: unlike them, I was losing mine. Theirs was a shiny, dark brown. The flea searcher, and not her alone, was interested in my face as well. The macaques' fingertips, to my surprise, are as soft as our own. I was enjoying the attention, it seemed like affection, but kept to my policy of passive participation in what was otherwise a lively occasion. No fleas were discovered, to my amused relief, perhaps to the monkey's disappointment. Then, suddenly, all of the monkeys were off, something urgent to attend to back in the forest – their curiosity abruptly satisfied. Mine was satisfied too.

We'd see them elsewhere on the island, mostly at a distance, but they were no competition for a movie star. Where were we in Bali? I forget exactly. It doesn't matter: if you are famous you can get mobbed and shrieked at anywhere. It was another leafy, off-the-street situation. A hoard of excited, young Japanese tourists had spotted a tall Caucasian couple: us. Or rather, it transpired, one of us in particular. For the Japanese, Bali was suddenly out of focus. We were surrounded. I'd never thought of the Japanese as being wildly spontaneous. Polite, well-mannered, reserved, yes. In the final decades of the twentieth century, they'd moved on from there. The woman they saw was elegant, tall, dark-eyed – well, I can't say exactly in what way she exemplified Western beauty to them but one thing was made clear: they knew she was a movie star, a celebrity. In response, and at a time when the media and public were becoming increasingly mass fixated on the lives of celebrities, crazy about them, the Japanese tourists were energetically curious. It made my meeting with the monkeys look tame, though not without correspondence. Luckily, the encounter with fame and the famous – who sop up without a squeeze so much unemployed, sedentary curiosity – was cauterised by the language problem. Most of the communication, from the Japanese tourists, was in any case definitely pre-language. I don't think we decided if the harsh truth would ever hit them that the woman they adored was not a movie star. Possibly not: like them, I'd become an extra in this sudden drama, that is, until I became the official photographer – and, what the hell, they were having, and were themselves, lots of fun. I could see through the lenses of the several cameras I focussed how much shorter than the willowy star the fans were, all of them beaming. Now that they had evidence of their remarkable encounter, they were happy to let Bali return to their lively attention – and remarked perhaps how proud I must be to again be at the side of a star. It was all very curious, this encounter over nearly as quickly as mine with the monkeys.

Harmless curiosity, we say approvingly, and can think of plenty that isn't when it becomes intrusive, interfering, prurient, sadistic, the list goes on, each kind often allied to some form of obsession. The borders of healthy curiosity may be uncertain. I can say with confidence – with a bow to Montaigne – I've come to admire curiosity in others as much or more than other admired qualities. Since all inquiry into the world around us began when we lived in forests and caves, and remains grounded in our surroundings we, if we are fortunate, can get overriding satisfactions wherever we are, like the Japanese tourists when they spotted their star and her lucky companion.

Not long ago, a weekend volunteer at Toronga Park Zoo in Sydney engaged the interest of a two-year-old boy. The man was roaming about a thoroughfare with a small eucalyptus branch and, seeing that the adults accompanying the boy were encouraging, offered him a closer look. Leaves! Except that, on much closer inspection, one of them turned out not to be part of the branch, though it was hardly distinguishable from the leaves. It was a perfectly camouflaged, slow-moving leaf insect – with a similar evolutionary trajectory to the better known stick insects. The considerate volunteer saw how absorbed the boy had quickly become, now that he was no longer running about – especially when the man gently separated the creature from the branch and rested it in his open hand. He'd found a sudden audience of three – could see that the boy's mother, my daughter, and I were also fascinated. A leaf insect was new to all three of us, though who knows how many we might narrowly have missed seeing in trees. But it was the boy's behaviour which struck the volunteer as being worthy of comment. He didn't endeavour to prod the insect in the hope, perhaps, of more action, behaviour the volunteer said is usual in diminutive zoo goers. He didn't poke it like an instant owner. He wasn't inclined to interfere with it at all, simply wanted to look, absorbed, until he was satisfied and ready to move on to see the big stars of the zoo. Stars! Our hierarchy. He'd just as good as seen one – his curiosity harmless.

# APPENDIX

The poems I write, my 'stock-in-trade', have always been largely incidental. The following pieces, about two of my poems, were requested. The first was written for *The Elizabeth Bishop Newsletter* (edited by Brian Bartlett, Nova Scotia, 2010) and the second for *Notes for the Translators* (edited by Christopher Kelen, ASM Poetry, Macao, 2012).

On a bedroom wall in the house where Elizabeth Bishop lived as a child hangs a framed poem – on linen paper – that I wrote several months ago. It is about my visit to that house in Great Village in April 2006. The bedroom was little Elizabeth's.

Let me briefly explain how this came about. Great Village is a long way from where I normally live in Australia. But that April I got lucky. While on a speedy reading tour of the Maritime Provinces – wonderful new territory for me – I met the Halifax-based poet, Brian Bartlett. Our conversation must have drifted to matters relating to EB, especially her relationship with Nova Scotia. I had realised that in all likelihood I might never again be as close to Great Village as I was then but had not entertained the possibility, on this hurried tour, of visiting it, let alone gaining entry to EB's grandparents' house. Brian explained how this could be done.

As it happened, in a few days I was to join – via public transport – a couple of Canadian poets, David Manicom and David O'Meara, for a reading in Fredericton, New Brunswick. I learned they had a go-anywhere car which would next take the three of us back to Halifax. Great Village, I'd heard, my eyes widening, would be accessible along the way. Good companions, the two Davids didn't require any persuading to make the detour. It was such a wonderful thing for me to be in places I'd never previously conceived of visiting that I felt I bore a disproportionate amount of the excitement. I hoped to see a moose somewhere but my luck didn't extend that far.

The weather was changeable the afternoon we arrived in Great Village. I remember this because I waited for the sun to make its various appearances, through openings in the clouds, to take my photographs. It was drizzling when we arrived, sunny when we left. The three of us were shown into the house by Meredith and Robert Layton, holders of the key and with whom I'd previously made contact. The poem, which I called 'Marvel', gives some idea of the intensity of the experience.

Here it is.

> Unexpectedly, one morning, I'm being driven fast
> to Great Village, Nova Scotia, where as a kid
> Elizabeth Bishop lived – went into the clapboard house,
> went up to the little room where she slept, or tried to,
> the sleep of a nascent poet. While, downstairs,
> her grandparents snoozed by the Little Marvel Stove.
> Now forever gone! I looked down at the narrow bed,
> up at the skylight right above it, home
> of the travelling Milky Way, while nearby roamed
> – or soon would – the moose she'd see from a bus
> and, with a trans-continental pen, take a
> modest twenty years to make, suddenly, marvellous.

Why I wrote the little poem when I did, I don't know. I suppose poems find you rather than you find them. The circumstance was unique: I was enjoying a few glasses of wine one evening when I jotted it down. It's the only poem I've written while drinking alcohol. I emailed it sometime later to Sandra Barry – whom I'd met in Montreal where she explained her connection with the house – and it was her generous idea that it be placed on the bedroom wall. When I recall that it is there, I also recall the overwhelming surprise and delight I experienced on reading Sandra's reply. I couldn't imagine a poem of mine ever finding a better home.

'Marvel', *The Bicycle Thief & Other Poems* (Black Pepper, 2013)

## Saxophone in a Pawnbroker's Window

Lost days when cavernous notes
reverberated seismically into the night,
or rose like an exotic flower,
wild and potent, a soloist's territory,
far from eyes locked
on the instrument's price.

The neighbours wished for him
and his gleaming saxophone, a gig,
or frozen keys, glad to miss
the magic of his fingertips.

Now it's a mirror for peering
shoppers, madly skewed;
and at a stretch along its tube,
the street curves weirdly
where the saxophonist
lost control of the one bright
ally with any value –
a beacon among cold rings
and trinkets for him to brave
the crazy way back
to meet his own reflection,
just in time, and get the music out.

    I wrote this short poem when I was living in London, having seen a saxophone for sale in a pawnbroker's window in Camden Town. But the specific location is not mentioned in the poem because it isn't significant. As far as I was concerned, the pawnbroker could have been located in any busy city in any country. What affected me was that someone had to relinquish an item, and on this occasion a musical instrument, that may well have been of great personal value – in fact possibly an item of the highest possible personal value. The poem is of course somewhat dependent upon the reader having prior knowledge of how a pawnbroker operates. An item that is pawned to him for money, in fact a loan, can within a specified time be claimed back by the owner at the amount for which it was pawned plus interest. If the item was pawned in a situation of financial desperation – as I imagined with the saxophone – the likelihood of this happening might be small. The events involving the saxophonist in my poem are wholly imagined and based upon my wish that things would work out for the best.

In the first verse paragraph I endeavour to establish the potential power and beauty of the instrument when it is played, the rising and falling of the notes. The notes are 'cavernous' in the sense that they seem to come from a deep and dark cave-like, primal place. The notes reverberate 'seismically', in other words seem earth-shaking, as if into the depths of the night. They are 'exotic' in relation to the surroundings, though this isn't specified. I saw no need. An 'exotic flower' in this context would command attention. The fact that the notes are 'wild and potent' suggests lack of inhibition combined with sexual energy, even forcefulness, but attractively so here. The specified contrast is with the 'locked' eyes, imprisoned, if you like, by mercantile considerations.

The second verse paragraph is intended to be humorous in a low-key way. The saxophonist might think he's producing wonderful music and loves his instrument above all else (in his 'soloist's territory') but the neighbours hold a different view. What is 'magic' to him creates in the neighbours a wish for the keys to be 'frozen' ( made inactive as would any form of life in conditions that are uninhabitable and cold), or that the guy might get a 'gig', a paid or unpaid booking to play – somewhere else.

It is significant that the saxophone gleams, shines, is a mirror – obviously well cared for but also eye-catching, and this allows for the concentrated imagery of the third section of the poem. Everything now happens in relationship to the displayed instrument itself and in a single long sentence of run-on lines, which I intended should create dynamic energy. There's a lot at stake! The reflections of the shoppers are 'madly skewed' and eventually the saxophonist makes his 'crazy way back' (just in time) along the street that 'curves weirdly'. The curves of the saxophone are reflecting expressionistically a mad world of which, in the shop window, it has become the focus. The saxophonist too has 'lost control' but he's about to re-establish some control by redeeming his possession, his 'one bright ally' – his brilliant and loyal companion – even though the specified time for doing so must have passed, since it is now for sale. It's a 'beacon', in other words, very noticeable, a kind of guide leading him back, among 'cold' items in the window. 'Cold' suggests an abandonment and withdrawal of love for the other items. But the keys of the saxophone won't be frozen much longer. The saxophonist dramatically gets to the shop in time (it's implied that he's raised the money) and 'gets the music out'. Not literally, of course. For him it's what the wonderful instrument does when he plays it not – any longer! – what it is worth in terms of market value. The fact that the saxophonist meets 'his own reflection/just in time' (a distorted reflection it must be in an instrument that is the one thing with which he truly identifies), reinforces the sense of the saxophonist's desperation and that he may well be isolated, perhaps narcissistically so, a true soloist!

When 'Saxophone in a Pawnbroker's Window' was first published a few years ago, in an Australian newspaper, someone from one of the state Education Departments got in touch with me and asked if I would give permission for the poem to be used in a state-wide English exam at the end of the year. I agreed – mainly for mercantile reasons. A copy of the examination booklet was later sent to me. Students were asked a number of questions about the poem – asked to do something that I myself would not wish to do. In fact I felt pretty sure that had I been subjected to this task – though I'd written the poem, some of the questions seemed to be getting at things I didn't get – I might not have, like the saxophone, shined. Though I hope it's possible for the author to provide some illumination, if necessary.

'Saxophone in a Pawnbroker's Window', *Speed & Other Liberties*
(Salt Publishing, 2008)